The Miracle Sellers

By Susan Puzio

A look into the lives and the methods TV preachers use to get filthy rich

"But he shall say, I tell you, I know you not whence ye are; depart from me, all ye workers of iniquity."

Luke 13:27

Dedication

Dedicated to my Lord and Savior, Jesus Christ.

Also, to my fellow laborers in the vineyard, who love the truth of God's holy Word.

To all the publishers of literature exposing heresy, as we join together to finish the Reformation.

All Scripture quotations from the King James Bible

All rights reserved, No part of this book may be reproduced without the author's written permission.

Copyright © 2025
Susan Puzio

ISBN
978-1-882970-04-9

Library of Congress control number
2025906065

Printed in the United States of America

Contact the Author
susan@propheticnews.com

Table of Contents

Introduction…………………………………..1

Chapter One: The Beginning……………...3

Chapter Two: My Journey Through Seed Faith and Word of Faith Teachings………..5

Chapter Three: How I Escaped from False Teachers and Con Artist Preachers………15

Chapter Four: Oral Roberts, Richard and Lindsey Roberts……………………….20

Chapter Five: Kenneth Hagin……………31

Chapter Six: The Major and Minor False Teachers…………………………………..45

Chapter Seven: Mike Murdock…………..49

Chapter Eight: Rod Parsley……………..55

Chapter Nine: Jan Crouch………………..65

Chapter Ten: Paula White………………..80

Chapter Eleven: Juanita Bynum………...104

Chapter Twelve: Marilyn Hickey...........112

Chapter Thirteen: Kenneth and Gloria Copeland, Jesse Duplantis……………...118

Chapter Fourteen: Steve Munsey..........140

Chapter Fifteen: Todd Coontz…………..149

Chapter Sixteen: God TV……………….154

Chapter Seventeen: Daystar…………….162

Chapter Eighteen: TBN………………...181

Chapter Nineteen: The Word Network…200

Chapter Twenty: TCT and Golden Eagle Broadcasting……………………………204

Chapter Twenty-one: Toufik Benedictus "Benny" Hinn……………………….....208

Chapter Twenty-two: Morris and David Cerullo…………………………………219

Chapter Twenty-three: Robert Morris….239

Chapter twenty-four: Mike Bickle……...243

Chapter twenty-five: Glossary of Other Miracle Sellers…………………………247

Epilogue……………………………….....281

Acknowledgements……………………..291

End Notes………………………………292

Nine of the Richest Pastors in America...301

Twenty-two of the Largest Churches in America………………………………….302
largest churches

Salaries of Ministry Executives………..304

The Miracle Sellers

Introduction

I was born again in 1981 in Redstone, Colorado, and there I received a miraculous deliverance from a life of sin and deception. I was thirty-one years old, and God gave me a brand-new life.

> *"Therefore if any man be in Christ, he is a new creature: old things are passed away; behold, all things are become new."*
> *2 Corinthians 5:17*

It is hard for people to understand the born-again experience unless they too have asked Jesus Christ to change their life. I now understood the true meaning of the old hymn: "Amazing Grace, how sweet the sound that saved a wretch like me, I once was lost, but now am found, was BLIND, but now I see."

> *"Marvel not that I said unto thee, Ye must be born again!"*

John 3:7

The Lord is merciful, and after much repentance, I wanted to do something for Him. Everybody should know about this glorious "good news."

I was about to embark on a journey of faith, a journey of blessings, and a journey of many disappointments, but through it, all I've learned to trust in Jesus!

The Beginning

"Woe unto you, scribes and Pharisees, hypocrites! For ye make clean the outside of the cup and of the platter, but within they are full of extortion and excess."

Matthew 23:25

Seed faith, I first heard that term when I started to attend a "Word of Faith" church in Glenwood Springs, Colorado.

Shortly after my conversion, someone gave me the book by Oral Roberts about "seed faith" and the "seed" was sown in my heart that I could give money and get even more money in return. What a deal!

I became interested in the teachings of people like Kenneth Hagin, Kenneth and Gloria Copeland, Oral Roberts, Norvel Hayes, and Marilyn Hickey, who then had "Happy Church" in Denver, Colorado, among many other teachers and authors.

Up until that time, I was attending a small country church in Redstone, Colorado, where the pastor was a trained Baptist. They did warn me to be careful about stepping into the waters of Charismania or Word of Faith, as it was called.

I was determined to spy out the land of Pentecostal Christianity. Being so young in the Lord, I was like a sponge, and these new teachings were attractive to me. I loved being in church and the fellowship with the saints. I was in love with my first love, Jesus. The world was beautiful, and I was saved!!

Not only could Jesus save me from hell, but He could heal me, deliver me from devils, and make me rich and prosperous.

Chapter Two:
My Journey Through Seed Faith and Word of Faith Teachings

"Yea, they are greedy dogs which can never have enough, and they are shepherds that cannot understand: they all look to their own way, every one for his gain, from his quarter." Isaiah 56:11

I stopped attending the small country church and jumped into the Word of Faith, positive confession movement.

I became acquainted with Harrison House Publications, and at the time, it was owned by Buddy Harrison, who was married to Kenneth Hagin's daughter, Pat. (Buddy passed away some years later in 1998; he died sick of cancer.)

I purchased over a hundred books from this publishing house. My favorite author was

Kenneth Hagin, but I loved them all. I read in many of these books that I could use the words of my mouth to create my reality.

Sickness, no; poverty, no, Jesus gave me His Word, and I could wield it like a sword to defeat the devil and have what I say.

We could do greater works than Jesus; that's what we were told.

The Full Gospel Businessmen Association was having a convention in Phoenix, Arizona, so I drove from Glenwood Springs, Colorado, to Phoenix, Arizona, in faith, with nowhere to stay and very little money in my pocket, but I was going in faith!!

I attended the meeting the night I arrived, and I thought I had died and gone to heaven; the music and the preaching were just out of this world. I just loved it!!

I was invited to stay with a beautiful family until the convention was over; they gave me a PTL study Bible, which I still have today. Living by faith seemed to be so much fun.

I started tithing 10% of my income and sowing seeds of money, giving away cars, clothing, money, my time, and whatever I could do to practice what the prosperity preachers were teaching me.

Gloria Copeland spoke a house into existence, and I was going to believe for a house too. I started to receive so many personal prophecies about what a great ministry God was going to give me, and I was going to be just like Kathryn Kuhlman.

Life was so exciting. Nothing could stop me from pursuing my vision to preach the gospel and have a worldwide ministry.

I moved to Florida shortly thereafter, and the Lord provided a house for me to live in; yes, I was working at different jobs to earn money, but nothing interested me as much as preaching and teaching the Bible.

Kenneth and Gloria Copeland were coming to Dade City, Florida, and I was going there without a car. I believed that by the end of the night, someone was going to approach me with a car.

I sat there until almost everyone was gone, but no one gave me a car. Thank God I had the phone number of a sister in the Lord in Dade City; otherwise, I may have had to walk home. She picked me up and drove me home the next day. I was crushed. Ken and Gloria got cars. What was wrong with my faith??

I was paying "God" 10% of my money, in fear of being cursed by Him for non-payment. For the most part, the pastor was living large off the tithe money, and it was not the case for most of the congregation.

Occasionally, the pastor would bring in guest speakers who would encourage us to sow seeds or cash. Some would even give us a personal prophecy for a seed faith gift. The best and longest personal prophecies were given to the biggest givers.

We all waited with great expectation for our words to come to pass and for our thirty, sixty, or one hundredfold returns to come. The talk was of mansions, luxury cars, jets, tailor-made clothing, and large honorariums; whatever we could believe, we could receive, especially if we were sowing seeds into good ground or "anointed" men and women of God.

Some people were even writing faith checks, paying bills, or giving offerings without any money in the bank to cover the check. I saw people give away everything they owned: houses, cars, jewelry, clothing; some were left devastated when the promised return did not come.

While in Florida, I would travel to Crystal River, where Norvel Hayes had a motel and a church building, and he would occasionally hold conferences there. Norvel was a Bible teacher who sometimes spoke at the Kenneth Copeland conventions. He was also a close friend of Kenneth Hagin.

He would bring in people like Rod Parsley, Robert Tilton, and many other Word of Faith teachers. It was always a small gathering of a few hundred people. We had many happy times in the Lord there. I was especially touched when Norvel Hayes called me out of a crowd at a Church of God service and gave me a personal prophecy. I was on cloud nine, and nothing could stop me from my destiny.

In the early 1980s, I attended a special summer school of Ministry at New Life Bible College in Cleveland, Tennessee, and in the early 1990s, I went to live and work on a volunteer basis at New Life, in Cleveland, Tennessee, where Norvel had a church and a Bible college.

I taught rarely at the Bible college, was the singles' minister, and also taught a Sunday school class. At that time, I was already traveling some and holding miracle healing services around the country. I was introduced to many ministries while I was there, which helped me to get open doors for ministry, especially in England.

I went back to Colorado somewhere around 1985 for a few years, where I produced and hosted a gospel television program for two years, which was broadcast in Aspen and Denver. It was there that I was introduced to Roberts Liardon; he was a guest on one of my programs, and I was later licensed and ordained under his ministry.

I was also a guest speaker at some of the singles' conferences held at Happy Church, where Wally and Marilyn Hickey were the pastors. I was a guest speaker at some Women's Aglow meetings and at various churches around the United States and in many foreign countries.

I always tried to pray for the sick, as I believed and still believe that Jesus is a healer and a miracle worker. Being young in the Lord, I made a lot of mistakes, but my heart was pure before God as far as doing the work of the ministry. I did not demand anything to come and preach, going on a freewill offering basis.

I never got into the seed faith, miracle-selling offering scam myself, although, for the most part, I was surrounded by that teaching. It worked for most of the ministries and was very lucrative. It seemed as though people enjoyed being manipulated.

We were people of faith, and we bound the spirit of fear, yet when it came to God, we were afraid of Him when it came to "His" money.

We faith people were scared to death of God, lest we not give Him His share. We stood waving our dollar bills at God, demanding that He bless us.

We were not in the habit of asking, but of demanding, using His Word over and over again until we got the desired result.

We were told giving was an act of worship, yet God calls money "filthy lucre." Now I can't imagine God being impressed with people waving money at him. Nobody ever did it to Jesus while He was on the earth.

Looking back now, I realize how foolish I was. It wasn't until I sat myself down over a three-month period in 1997, and as I studied all the scriptures on giving, tithing, and seed sowing, I found out the truth about it all.

Money was never seed, tithing was never money, and giving was an act of love. God would never bless selfishness or giving just to get something in return.

For God so loved the world that He gave!!

I published a newsletter that year titled "The Error of Seed Faith Giving." It was the nail in the coffin for my ministry as I knew it. I would never again receive an invitation to a "Word of Faith" church.

I took myself out of public ministry for many years, refusing to do ministry the way that I knew it.

Re-emerging with a website in early 2004 or so, then in 2009, I began a radio broadcast on Blog Talk Radio, which is an internet radio platform. We are now heard on Spreaker. We have since expanded our outreach to many other social media venues. This has proven to be a tremendous blessing, as God has blessed us with thousands of listeners. Hungry hearts, also tired of church as we knew it.

The church has become a laughingstock to the world, as Christians are portrayed on television and other platforms as greedy manipulators, selling miracles for seed faith gifts.

Chapter 3:
How I Escaped from False Teachers and Con Artist Preachers

"Having eyes full of adultery and that cannot cease from sin; beguiling unstable souls: an heart they have exercised with covetous practices; cursed children."

2 Peter 2:14

I made my escape from the false teachers, false prophets, and the ungodly, uncaring manipulators who rob widows' houses and are not ashamed to come into your house via radio, television, and the computer to rob you using hypnotism and witchcraft.

They promise you healing, financial miracles, household salvation, debt cancellation, a year of jubilee blessing, the fifty-eight-dollar blessing, the thousand-dollar seed offering, and the 24/7 miracle;

wow, they stay up late at night thinking of gimmicks. They are talented Baal worshipers.

I am going to say it; how can you be born again and Holy Ghost-filled and act like a reprobate? The greedy bunch of hypocrites who lie about Jesus cannot be saved.

The Holy Spirit brings conviction, but they long ago quit listening to the convicting power of the Holy Ghost, if they ever heard Him at all. The greedy miracle sellers enjoy the WAGES of sin!

They like the praises of men, the bodyguards, the jets, the mansions, the tailor-made clothes, the Rolex watches, the drugs, the alcohol, the adultery, the homosexuality, whatever work of the flesh that gratifies them.

They are not ministers of the Lord Jesus Christ as they continue to bring a reproach to His holy name.

Do they really believe people are going to hell without the saving knowledge of Jesus Christ? Because if they did, they would turn from their wicked ways.

And to the sheep of His pasture, run for your lives from these people. Run out the door screaming: HELP!!

Quit supporting them with your time and money; you are responsible for reading your Bible and then acting accordingly. They only survive because of your financial support.

Let the Reformation begin again!

Martin Luther posts his ninety-five theses
protesting selling time out of purgatory,
among other offensive religious practices.

Chapter 4

Oral Roberts

"Or who hath first given to him and it shall be recompensed unto him again?"

Romans 11:35

Oral Roberts, some say that he is the father of the seed faith movement. Oral knew a good thing when he found it or said it in his case.

He lived a lavish lifestyle with the seed faith offerings of many of the poor and needy people that he fleeced. Someone said these people sell hope, and how true that is.

Oral was born in Oklahoma in 1918 to a poor family and almost died of tuberculosis at the age of seventeen. He said he was put into a car, and they drove him to a healing meeting, where he was prayed for, and then God healed him; he was also healed of stuttering.

Oral was a pastor before he became a healing evangelist, but soon after, he started his famous tent crusades, where he would lay hands on the thousands who attended; his tent could seat up to 12,000 people.

Oral became a fixture on television in the 1950s, one of the first to televise his healing services.

I remember turning on the TV and seeing him praying for the sick when I was about nine or 1ten. My mom said, "Oh, that's not real." (I was raised Catholic, and God couldn't do much of anything for us.) I didn't pay him any attention at the time. It was not until the 1980s when I was given a copy of his book that I learned about seed faith. The book was *The Miracle of Seed Faith*, and it was then that I became acquainted with Oral Roberts.

What a deal it was. I was to give "God money" (or Oral in this case), and God Almighty Himself was then obligated to return it unto me thirty, sixty, or one hundredfold.

I must admit, at the time, the book seemed a little like some of the New Age teachings that I had heard when I made one of my journeys looking for Jesus through that movement. But, at the time, because he was an anointed, respected man of God in my circles, and he wrapped his teachings with scriptures, who was I to question the great, successful Oral Roberts?

I went to a Miracle Healing Crusade in Madison Square Garden in New York City, and I cannot remember the year, but both Richard and Oral Roberts were praying for the thousands of people who filled the arena. I was very impressed with the service. I loved basking in that atmosphere of music, preaching, and miracles.

Sometime in the late 1980s, I traveled to Tulsa-rusalem to see the new City of Faith Hospital. I also visited Oral Roberts

University, built in 1963, and attended a Rhema camp meeting, which I will talk about later in my chapter about Kenneth Hagin.

The City of Faith Hospital was a good idea, nothing wrong with merging prayer and medicine. Why it went bankrupt, I do not know. I can only speculate about the reasons. Mismanagement, greed? The famous praying hands sculpture now sits on the campus of ORU, which bears the Roberts' name, but no longer belongs to them.

Just about everything the Roberts family built no longer belongs to them. Oral died in 2009, and Richard Roberts was the heir apparent; his mismanagement plunged the university to over $50,000,000 in debt, or maybe he inherited the debt from seed faith ain't working for the Roberts family, Oral.

Anyway, seed faith did not work for them; they took in hundreds of millions of dollars, only to lose most of it.

Richard and Lindsey moved to Florida after a series of embarrassing incidents in Tulsa, such as Richard driving over ninety miles an hour and being arrested for drunk driving, and Lindsey had her own set of problems. They now reside in Texas, where they are still busy collecting millions of dollars in seed faith offerings.

By the way, the former Mrs. Richard Roberts, Patti, wrote a blockbuster book in 1983, *Ashes to Gold*, chronicling the jet-set lifestyle of the rich and famous Roberts family. I have read this book, and I highly recommend it. She compared Oral to Johann Tetzel, a Catholic who sold time out of purgatory for offerings. (The Catholic church still does this.) That's one of the ways St. Peter's in Rome was built. The Roberts empire was built in a similar fashion.

Some fired faculty members of ORU filed lawsuits and brought up some nasty charges; the suit was settled, and it went away, or the Roberts family paid them off to silence them.

It just seems to me if you are innocent, why do you settle lawsuits and require confidentiality?

Here are some quotes from a published news story from CNN.com published on October 16th, 2007:

"The new allegations come in an amended version of the wrongful termination suit filed by three former professors, who say they lost their jobs after reporting that Roberts and his family lavishly spent school money for personal expenses."

"The amended lawsuit, filed Friday, also alleges that the university gave a 'convicted sexual deviant unrestricted access to students' while the man acted as a 'mentor.' The lawsuit also claims the university shredded evidence three days after the suit was filed against the school. The school denies both accusations in a statement on its Web site."

Some facts about ORU:
It sits on 263 acres.
Founded by Oral Roberts in 1963, who died at age ninety-one in Dec. 2009.
Richard Roberts resigned in 2007 or was forced out. Had a $50,000,000 debt in 2007.

Former City of Faith Hospital, Tulsa, Oklahoma

Hobby Lobby's Green family now owns it. They reportedly gave over 100 million dollars to retire debt and to renovate the property.

ORU also owns the GEB Television network, which features different pimp preachers at the Mabee Center, who then teach gullible college students how to learn the art of seed faith sowing to get God to do what they want. What a thing to teach young people.

Quote from a book by Jerry Sholes, *Gimme that Prime Time Religion*, published in 1979:

> "The finances of Oral Roberts' ministry as Sholes related that Oral Roberts' mail room is equipped to handle 20,000 letters per day. He related that 90% of those letters contain a contribution and the average contribution is $5.00. The daily income of the Oral Roberts' ministry from the mail room alone would tally $90,000 pcr day or $450,000 per week. This comes to $23,400,000 per year from mailroom contributions alone (p. 8)."

The Roberts family had their own set of tragedies. In 1982, Oral's son Ronald, age thirty-seven, committed suicide with a single gunshot to the heart. A daughter, Rebecca, and her husband, Marshall, were killed in a plane crash in 1997, and Richard and Lindsey had a baby boy who died two days after birth.

Now Richard and Lindsey have a television broadcast where they always have a way of getting you to sow a financial seed to them.

They complain people say bad things about them, but maybe they should take some of those things to heart. Miracle selling was responsible for the rise and fall of the Roberts ministry, and selling miracles is hardly a ministry that would be associated with our Lord, Jesus Christ.

Richard Roberts' mug shot from his drunk driving arrest

Oral Roberts University

Tulsa, OK • Tax-exempt since Jan. 1964 • EIN: 73-0739626

 Receive an email when new data is available for this organization.

Type of Nonprofit

Designated as a 501(c)3

Organizations for any of the following purposes:

Revenue
$192M (2022)

Expenses
$146M (2022)

Income for ORU 2022

Oral Roberts Evangelistic Association

Tulsa, OK | EIN: 73-0568096 | 501(c)(3) Public Charity

Total revenue: Total assets: Total giving:

$5,506,935 $7,403,778 $554,426

Year 2023 Richard Roberts is the Oral Roberts Evangelistic Association/his income

Chapter Five:
Kenneth E. parsley

"And as it is appointed unto men once to die, but after this the judgment."

Hebrews 9:27

Hagin was called the father of the faith movement and the founder of Rhema Bible Training Center in Tulsa, Oklahoma. He died sick of heart disease. He could not confess it away. The reports say he collapsed at home, which is usually caused by heart failure, and he died in a cardiac intensive care unit. Kenneth Erwin Hagin (August 20, 1917 – September 19, 2003)

The irony of it is that he taught that Christians should not die sick; we could confess our way out of sickness, but it did not work for Kenneth E. Hagin.

We are not failures because we get sick or die sick; we get the ultimate healing when we die. To be absent from the body is to be present with the Lord.

I never heard of anyone confessing they wanted cancer, yet "Word of Faith" people say, "Oh, he or she must have had a bad confession, or they must have sin in their life." We were the most uncompassionate bunch going. We were the love people, yet we looked down on the sick. Oh, and if someone died sick, we blamed them for dying; yes, we believed in heaven, but if anyone went there, we were upset that they died of an illness. Even though the Bible says it is appointed by a sovereign God to die.

Hagin wrote over a hundred books, especially on healing. I had almost every book he ever wrote. I especially liked the books about his visions of seeing Jesus and Jesus talking with him. Hagin claimed Jesus appeared to him personally about eight times. He seemed to have an inside contact with the Almighty that the average person did not have.

Here are some of the accounts of his visits with Jesus taken from D.R. McConnell's book, *A Different Gospel* (p. 64):

Hagin: "Then the Lord said this to me, which is not just for my benefit, but for yours, 'If you will learn to follow that inward witness, I will make you rich.'"

"I am not opposed to my children being rich. I am opposed to their being covetous. I have followed that inward witness and He has made me rich." (p. 32, *How You Can Be Led by the Spirit of God*, Kenneth E. Hagin)
I attended a few of his healing meetings, and at one of those meetings, you had to fill out a card before he would pray for you.

You could not just go up into the healing line. I wondered, *What if a really sick person came in late and did not fill out the card? Could they still get prayed for?* Although I was excited to be there, Hagin's style of preaching was not what I had imagined it to be; it was a bit dull. But after all, it was the "anointed" Kenneth Hagin with healing in his hands that should have been enough.

When I traveled to Tulsa-rusalem in the late 1980s, I attended a Kenneth Hagin camp meeting. All of a sudden, Kenneth and Gloria Copeland were coming in the front door. Gloria looked beautiful in her full-length mink coat, perfect make-up, and hairstyle. They were friendly, and they smiled and said hello as they entered. So many "anointed" men and women of God were there.

I was staying with a friend I had met in Florida and her family. I did not know it at the time, but she was suffering from emotional problems and at times would exhibit strange behavior.

I later learned that she was banned from attending the camp meeting. I wondered why because this ministry was famous for casting out devils, and the City of Faith was there also. Couldn't anyone cast the devil out of her? Couldn't the great City of Faith take her in for treatment?

Then I saw it with my own eyes. I was at the camp meeting one night, and right when Hagin stood up to preach, my friend came barreling through the door, and she ran up to Hagin, shouting something. Wow, I was shocked; the ushers jumped up and carried her out the door, dragging her under her arms. There was no casting out devils, there was no prayer from all the greats, and she was kicked out!!

That left a lasting impression on me. I never looked at Kenneth Hagin the same again. After I got delivered from the Word of Faith mess in the late 1990s, I got rid of all my Kenneth Hagin books. I did not want them in my house.

Someone gave me a copy of the book, *A Different Gospel* by D.R. McConnell; the book shows the correlation between the Word of Faith movement and metaphysics among other relevant topics. It was originally his master's thesis, "The Kenyon Connection: A Theological Analysis of the Cultic Origins of the Faith Movement," which was submitted to the faculty of the School of Theology at Oral Roberts University in 1982. (quote from his book, preface)

I would not read it for the longest time; it was a gift from a friend, but finally, I did. I was shocked to learn of the cultic origins of what I had believed. I could not deny his findings, and I knew he was telling the truth about Hagin plagiarizing E.W. Kenyon, which Kenneth Hagin denied, but it was word for word in some instances.

McConnell also talks about the born-again Jesus and faith in faith; we were great at that. We ordered God around, telling Him or reminding Him, as they say, of what He should do for us.

Here are some of the writings of Hagin versus Kenyon for comparison.

Kenneth Hagin" "The 22nd Psalm gives a graphic picture of the crucifixion of Jesus—more vivid than that of John, Matthew, or Mark who witnessed it."

E.W. Kenyon: "The twenty-second Psalm gives a graphic picture of the crucifixion of Jesus. It is more vivid than that of John, Matthew, or Mark who witnessed it."

Here is a quote from Kenyon's daughter: "They've [the Faith teachers] all copied from my Dad [E. W. Kenyon]. They've changed it a little bit and added their own touch... but they couldn't change the wording. The Lord gave him [Kenyon] words and phrases. He coined them. They can't put it in any other words... It's very difficult for some people to be big enough to give credit to somebody else." (Ruth Kenyon Houseworth, taped interview, Lynnwood, WA, Feb. 19, 1982)

Kenneth Hagin quotes: "Man is a spirit who possesses a soul and lives in a body. He is in the same class with God. We know that God is a Spirit. And yet [He] took upon Himself a man's body. When God took upon Himself human form, He was no less God than when He didn't have a body. Man, at physical death, leaves his body. Yet he is no less man than he was when he had his body. (*Man of Three Dimensions*, Tulsa: Faith Library, 1973, no page)

E.W. Kenyon: "Man is a spirit being, he has a soul, and he lives in a body. He is in the same class as God. We know that God is a spirit and He became a man and took on a man's body, and when He did it, He was no less God than He was before He took the physical body... Man, at death, leaves his physical body and is no less man than he was when he had his body (*The Hidden Man*, Seattle: Kenyon's Gospel Publishing Society, 1970, p. 40; *Two Kinds of Faith*, p. 3)

I highly recommend reading this book. The research is excellent. Kenyon studied metaphysics in his early years, and it is reflected in his teachings. Some of it was related to the New Thought teachings of people like Phineas P. Quimby, Emerson College, the Unity School of Christianity, and Mary Baker Eddy, the founder of Christian Science.

"Another accusation of plagiarism arose from Dale Simmons, a graduate of ORU, who in 1983 discovered as much as 75% of Hagin's Authority of the Believer booklet, was taken word for word from articles published in 1932 by John A. MacMillan under the same title." (*A Different Gospel*, D.R. McConnell, p. 69) This also was denied by Hagin when he was confronted with it.

The most important contradiction I believe, concerning Hagin, is his deathbed testimony. Here he claims he dies several times or leaves his body as his heart stops; he is unsaved, and he goes down to the gates of hell, but he is born again after the third time as he goes down to the gates and then goes back into his body.

I do not believe you can die, go to hell, and come back. Hell is permanent; you don't get another chance. Maybe his clever use of words, "I did not lose consciousness-my heart stopped beating (I think when your heart stops beating, you do lose consciousness), I left my body," can be a distraction to what he is saying, or what is he really trying to say?

He sure could spin a tall tale in a folksy manner. Here are some quotes from Hagin's testimony. (I went to hell-YouTube)
"I Went To Hell" | Rev. Kenneth E. Hagin's Experience (Reenacted)

"My heart stopped beating. This numbness spread to my feet, my ankles, my knees, my hips, my stomach, and my heart and I leaped out of my body.

"I did not lose consciousness; I leaped out of my body like a diver would leap off a diving board into a swimming pool. I knew I was outside my body. I could see my family in the room, but I couldn't contact them."

He then claims that when he gets to the gates of hell, he does not go in but is sucked back up into his body.

"My heart stopped for a second time. I leaped out of my body and began to descend: down, down, down. Oh, I know it was just for a few seconds, but it seemed like an eternity.

"The farther down I went, the hotter and darker it became, until I came again to the bottom of the pit and saw the entrance to hell, or the gates as I call it. I was conscious that that creature met me.

"It was like suction to my back. I never turned around. I just came floating back into the shadows of darkness. And then I was pulled up, head first. I could see the lights of the earth above me before I came up out of the pit. The only difference this time was that I came up at the foot of the bed. For a second time, I stood there. I could see my body lying there on the bed. I could see Grandma as she sat there holding me in her arms.

"I could feel the circulation as it cut off. Suddenly my toes went numb. Faster than you can snap your fingers, my toes, feet, ankles, knees, hips, stomach and heart went dead and I leaped out of my body and began to descend."

He claims he was born again the third time when he re-entered his body. The full story can be seen on the internet, or you can read it in Hagin's book, *I Went to Hell.*

There also is a very disturbing video of Hagin sticking his tongue out like a snake, and the people seem hypnotized by him as they fall down and act like they just came from an insane asylum, including Kenneth Copeland.

Hagin himself cannot stand up, and at one point, he falls as others try to hold him up. He was already a much older man at this time. Joseph Chambers of Paw Creek Ministries produced an excellent video about this, *Kenneth Hagin, Spirit of the Serpent.*

Kenneth Hagin's son Ken has a television program, and he now runs the ministry along with his wife, Lynette.

Ken Jr. pastors the Rhema Church in Tulsa; it looks like he can still draw a crowd. Rhema Bible Training Center is still operating. It was once the premier place to go for "Word of Faith" Bible teaching.

On page 75 in D.R. McConnell's book, "A Different Gospel" there is one resurrection account, of a prominent member of Hagin's church who died and went to heaven. Not willing to release the man who had been a Sunday school teacher and gave 20% of his income to the church, Hagin prayed earnestly for the man's life.

As the man later described it to Hagin, upon his arrival in heaven, he was met by Jesus himself, who told him, "You're going to have to go back." Jesus was said to have replied apologetically, "Brother Hagin won't let you come yet." Hagin claims this is an example of the authority of his intercession. (see Kenneth Hagin, *Plead Your Case*)

Wow, he had some kind of supposed power even over Jesus!! Yet, no one could call him, Kenneth Hagin, back, and he died just like the rest of us, and his mortal remains lie in a mausoleum at Floral Havens Memorial Gardens, Broken Arrow, Oklahoma.

Chapter Six:
The Major and Minor False Teachers and Miracle Sellers

"And the elders of Moab and the elders of Midian departed with the rewards of divination in their hand; and they came unto Balaam, and spake unto him the words of Balak."

Numbers 22:7

The major false prophets have spawned a new breed of imitators who know a good scam when they see it. Most are biblically uneducated and without any personal ambition except to be a pimp preacher.

That is easy; just hold up a Bible and tell people what they want to hear, especially that they can be rich without working for it.

Debts? Oh, you don't have to pay them; you can have debt cancellation.

I recently heard a "church" go crazy when they were told to sow their seed for debt cancellation. Now how could a holy, righteous God cancel your debts, and the person you owe the money to gets robbed?

The only way to get your debts canceled is to file for bankruptcy or to get the person to forgive your debts personally.

A well-known false prophet even claimed he was out of debt miraculously; what he forgot to say was he filed for bankruptcy, and both his church properties were in foreclosure.

One was sold before the auction, the other was sold to the creditor at the foreclosure auction, and they still owed millions. He even went on national TV boasting about his miracles. Which just goes to show you can't believe too much of what these people tell you. They don't mind lying, even about God.

The next few chapters will be dedicated to the major players of the day and the minor ones. Just turn on "Christian" TV, and the airways are full of these sellers of miracle spring water, holy oil, and with the swami and his predictions of the blessings that will come your way for the $1,000 seed.

These charlatans will never be satisfied. Greed is ugly. As the Bible says, what does it profit a man to gain the whole world and lose his own soul?

Pharaoh disobeyed, and it cost him much suffering!

Let my people go!!

Chapter Seven:
Mike Murdock

"Her princes in the midst thereof are like wolves ravening the prey, to shed blood, and to destroy souls, to get dishonest gain."

Ezekiel 22:27

As I was flipping through the channels one night, there was Mike; he was on three different television networks simultaneously. Sometimes he looked like he had just gotten out of bed, or he had been on a long drunk. He looked rough.

I wonder how he ever gets to sleep at night, thinking about all the various prosperity scams he is running as the great Dr. Mike. The $58 blessing, the $1,000 seed, the millionaire club, etc., etc. Mike loves to brag about all his cars, jewelry, houses, and airplanes, all his ill-gotten gains.

A book was written about Dr. Mike by someone who had access to his home and closet through his adopted son. It was alleged that his closet was full of other people's jewelry and valuable coins, taken from the gullible sheep, along with unmentionable magazines and unclean homemade videos of his female conquests.

The author documented the immorality of Mike Murdock, and he was never sued for defamation or slander. It is not so hard to see that Mike is in trouble, big trouble with God.

He is a favorite at telethon time, the greedy gospel merchants jumping with glee as Mike rakes in the cash so that their "God" can be blessed with filthy lucre.

Their god must have cold hard cash, or he cannot get his gospel out, and it sometimes must be delivered in corporate jets, with the use of mega-mansions, while driving a Rolls Royce or a Bentley or staying in a presidential suite while wearing an Armani suit and a solid gold Rolex watch, with butlers, maids, armor bearers, and whatever they can purchase by lying and manipulating.

Of course, people in full-time ministry should be paid, but for the most part, the person on top of the pyramid scheme is the one reaping the promised harvest.

Mike says "precious friends" and no, you are not his precious friend. He only loves you for what he can get from you.

"A good man obtaineth favour of the LORD: but a man of wicked devices will he condemn."
Proverbs 12:2

Mike says, "Seed guarantees divine favor. Your seed creates a covenant with God. Expect uncommon wisdom, and the greatest financial break-through ever."

I already have divine favor. I already have a covenant with God. I can pray for wisdom; it is free for the asking. I can pray, and God said that He would meet my needs. Mike hopes that you will never read your Bible; you might find him out!

"And delivered him out of all his afflictions, and gave him favour and wisdom in the sight of Pharaoh king of Egypt; and he made him governor over Egypt and all his house."
Acts 7:10

No one here sent seed faith gifts to get favor; it was freely given!

Mike has no respect for the body of Christ; he must think us all fools!

"The words of wise men are heard in quiet more than the cry of him that ruleth among fools."
Ecclesiastes 9:17

God is my Father, my loving heavenly Father. I don't need to give Murdock any seed faith gift to get God to hear my prayers. Is he really born again? This is not the Holy Spirit of Jesus Christ, but an anti-Christ spirit. Anti-everything Jesus Christ teaches.

Notice the artful manipulation in this statement: "The size of your seed always determines the size of your harvest." In other words, send me a big fat check!

The god of Mike Murdock sits on his throne with an angry look on his face, and we must lay money at his feet or wave it in his face to get him to perform. His god hates love and compassion. His god loves selfish motives. His god has children who only do things for others if they are going to cash in.

What kind of Christianity is that? It flies in the face of the words of Jesus, who said we are to love our neighbor as we love ourselves; we are to give, expecting nothing in return; we are to be lovers, the way God loved, to the point where He gave His only begotten Son. Does any of that pertain to Mike and his $58 blessing? They even turn the birth of Jesus into seed sowing, saying God sowed His Son. The blasphemy never ends.

"Wherefore is there a price in the hand of a fool to get wisdom, seeing he hath no heart to it?"
Proverbs 17:16

"Buy the truth, and sell it not; also wisdom, and instruction, and understanding."
Proverbs 23:23

Mike came to a church that I attended in 1996, and he had the $58 blessing that day, instructing us to write on our checks what we wanted God to do for us.

One lady stood up to testify about how God gave her a husband when she sowed a $58 seed. They both stood up, beaming about their marriage, which later ended with the husband being arrested for fraud, going to prison, and leaving the wife bankrupt, and divorce soon followed. I guess you get what you pay for!

Chapter 8
Rod Parsley

"Then the LORD said unto me, The prophets prophesy lies in my name: I sent them not, neither have I commanded them, neither spake unto them: they prophesy unto you a false vision and divination, and thing of naught, and the deceit of their heart."

Jeremiah 14:14

It must be mighty expensive to be Rod Parsley these days. He is on television daily and is paying huge sums of money for airtime as he presents to you a new miracle buying, seed faith scheme almost every day. There are Passover offerings, first fruits, resurrection seeds, Pesach Sheni, etc. Rod's got it down, or so he thinks.

What happened to the guy who just wanted to see a soul saved? Gone is the innocence and the charisma that made him famous. I was in a gospel meeting with Rod. In the early days, I must say he seemed like a nice enough brother with his dramatic flair and his overemphasized use of words. It made him a crowd favorite.

It got a little weird when I saw someone wearing a lampshade in one of the televised services, and more weirdness followed as time went on.

In the late 1980s, I was trying to purchase a TV license to start a Christian television station in Colorado. We were going to sell the airtime for $50 an hour. Yes, I said $50.

Anyway, Rod was preaching near my home, and I went to hear him. After the service, I went to speak with him to ask him if he wanted to be on our network. He said to talk to Clint (Clint Brown); he was his worship leader. I asked Clint if they wanted to help reach the lost in Aspen, Colorado, just $50 an hour for the time. "Oh," he said, "we would have to do a market study first to see if it's feasible."

I could not believe what I was hearing. A market study for $50? I was so naive at the time, and I thought they were really interested in preaching the gospel to the lost, but they weren't. I knew then that Rod Parsley was headed for trouble.

Too much, too soon? Or who really is Rod Parsley? He seems like a man on a mission, a mission to destroy any last bit of integrity he ever had as a minister of the gospel.

Did it get to be too much for Rod to try to keep the monster he created fed? The television bills, the mega church, the lawsuits, and the debts can mount up fast. Then there is the ego.

When Rod came to the crossroads in his ministry, it seemed as though he cracked and sold out. Any of us who tried full-time ministry knew that we had a way with crowds. We can sway a crowd. You can use it for good, or you can crack and use it for your own gain. The Bible talks about cunning craftiness.

> *"That we henceforth be no more children tossed to and fro, and carried about with every wind of doctrine, by the sleight of men, and cunning craftiness, whereby they lie in wait to deceive."*
> *Ephesians 4:14*

It becomes just like that when you sell out and begin to use manipulation; it becomes cunning and crafty. That's why it's called witchcraft. You use your craft to manipulate, to use God and the Lord Jesus Christ as a prop to sell your product.

Rod started a school that was called Valor, to train young people for the ministry, yet Rod sets a very poor example for them to follow. He does not teach them to seek first the Kingdom of God or to live by faith; he teaches them by example to be a miracle seller to fund their ministries.

To have a gimmick or a miracle to sell is an easy way to achieve what false prosperity preachers deem success, especially if it involves M-0-N-E-Y.

One of the saddest things that I ever heard Rod say was that he sowed a seed or gave "God" money to heal his autistic son. Why? If you really knew Jesus Christ, why would you lay down filthy money to God for a miracle? Is there one account in the Bible, one, where Jesus Christ, the God of our salvation, our blessed Lord, accepted money to answer someone's prayer? Rod and his partner in crime, "Miss Joni," laid down the money at his altar at World Harvest Church, giving it to himself. Selfish to the end. Where do they get this nonsense from?

Rod now hosts most of the other puppet masters on his television program, *Breakthrough*, such as the likes of Todd

Coontz, who acts like he was a used car salesman in a previous era. Then there is George Bloomer, who will sweat on your money so that you will receive his anointing and get some miracle money. George confessed to shooting up drugs while on the preaching circuit, and he said he is now delivered. Yet, I wonder with delusional talk like that, what is he still smoking?

And Clint, remember Clint Brown, the Parsley protégé? His church in Orlando, the former meeting place of "Pastor Benny Hinn," which Clint purchased after Hinn left town, was sold at a foreclosure auction in July 2014, owing some ten million dollars. Faith World is no more, and now Clint has a new church named Judah Church in Orlando.

This is what happened to King Nebuchadnezzar for not obeying God. He lost his mind and looked like a wild man.

"All this came upon the king Nebuchadnezzar. At the end of twelve

months, he walked in the palace of the kingdom of Babylon.

"The king spake, and said, Is not this great Babylon, that I have built for the house of the kingdom by the might of my power, and for the honour of my majesty? While the word was in the king's mouth, there fell a voice from heaven, saying, O King Nebuchadnezzar, to thee it is spoken; The kingdom is departed from thee. And they shall drive thee from men, and thy dwelling shall be with the beasts of the field: they shall make thee to eat grass as oxen, and seven times shall pass over thee, until thou know that the most High ruleth in the kingdom of men, and giveth it to whomsoever he will. The same hour was the thing fulfilled upon Nebuchadnezzar: and he was driven from men, and did eat grass as oxen, and his body was wet with the dew of heaven, till his hairs were grown like eagles' feathers, and his nails like birds' claws.

"And at the end of the days, Nebuchadnezzar lifted up mine eyes unto

heaven, and mine understanding returned unto me, and I blessed the most High, and I praised and honoured him that liveth forever, whose dominion is an everlasting dominion, and his kingdom is from generation to generation."
Daniel 4:28-34

The same fate will come upon Rod if it has not already. He seems like a man bent on destruction. Because of his pride and arrogance, the hammer of God's judgment could fall. How are the mighty fallen!

Here are some famous Parsley heresy quotes:

"$10,000 - God is speaking that to 34 people. Everybody else sow $1,000 if your need can be represented by a $1,000 seed! If you can't sow the whole $1,000 right now sow $500. and believe God for the other $500...But take a step of faith right now."

"'I just love to talk about money,' he told them. I just love to talk about your money.

Let me be very clear - I want your money. I deserve it. This church deserves it."
https://www.youtube.com/watch?v=D6CSHWd_dDE

Rod Parsley had a bout with throat cancer a few years back. He had received twenty-eight radiation treatments, and they were assessing the damage to his vocal cords. On September 13, 2015, Rod and his family appeared at his church, World Harvest. After being gone for ninety-one days from his pulpit, you could see that he had suffered, and he did not utter a word. There was a huge bandage covering his throat from radiation burns, along with a scruffy beard.

Throat cancer, big words. If God does not heal you, then it won't happen.

As of this writing, Rod has not changed. He has grown even more arrogant and full of pride. He now says he has a seven times greater anointing.

His daughter, Ashton, now helps with the ministry, calling herself the first daughter. She seems to be following in her father's footsteps and has not taken a stand against the miracle selling. In an interview, Ashton said she was going to commit suicide and that she had to take anti-anxiety medication. Why all the anxiety? After all, her father is Rod Parsley. Just maybe she would like to be just Ashton.

It would be great if Ashton could raise a new standard there of integrity. She could truly help to change her generation. There is so much pressure for the children of these people to take over their kingdoms, and just maybe they don't want to.

Chapter 9
Janice Bethany Crouch

"Bread of deceit is sweet to a man; but afterwards his mouth shall be filled with gravel."

Proverbs 20:17

Jan Crouch was one of the founders of TBN, Trinity Broadcasting Network, and the wife of the late Paul Crouch, who died of heart failure in 2013. Jan passed away in May 2016 at seventy-seven years of age.

Jan wore many hats or wigs at TBN, and she could be sweet, or she could be vicious. Just ask her grandchildren, Cara, Brittany, and Brandon, the children of Paul Crouch Jr., about Granny Dearest.

Jan fired her granddaughter Brittany, who was another one of the "heirs apparent" to the empire built on seed faith scams and spiritual pyramid schemes using Bible scriptures to get whatever their greedy minds desired.

Jan also had Paul Crouch Jr., her eldest son, fired, or as he says, he "resigned," but Jan and Matt wanted him out. Every last trace of that part of the family was eliminated, and their photos were removed from the walls of remembrance.

When Paul Sr. died, they were not invited to the memorial service, nor did they get to say their goodbyes according to public posts from Brandon, Brittany, and Cara, the grandchildren.

Matt Crouch, it was alleged by Brittany in an interview with Jackie Alnor, said that he was not the biological son of Paul. Matt would probably like all of them to stay away forever since now he will inherit that horrendous network, which has done more harm than good for the cause of Christ and made a laughingstock out of true biblical Christianity.

Here is a quote from the Orange County Register on June 8, 2012, about Brittany Crouch, daughter of Paul Crouch Jr.:

"Brittany, who worked for Trinity from 2007 to 2011, has accused the mighty Christian broadcaster of playing fast and loose with the ministry's millions and provided internal documents to back up her claims.

"She says it unlawfully distributed charitable assets worth more than $50 million to the company's directors (her family members); bought a $50 million jet through 'a sham loan to an alter ego corporation' for the personal use of the Crouches, as well as a $100,000 motor home that's used as a mobile residence for her grandmother's dogs; falsely reported 'multiple residential estates' as guest homes or church parsonages to avoid income disclosures; doled out meal expenses of up to a half-million dollars per company director;

paid personal chauffeurs with Trinity funds disguised as medical payments; and engaged in 'multiple cover- ups of sexual and criminal scandals.'" (Teri Sforza staff writer)

The harassment of Brittany did not stop there. Grandma Dearest accused her of stealing money from the ministry, but who are the real thieves here? The accusations were made after the memo was sent and the firings occurred.

Brittany, an MBA, was the chief financial officer and her then-husband was an attorney. What exactly was her "crime"?

From Wikipedia: "On August 30, 2011, Koper (name at the time) and her husband (a lawyer, also employed by TBN) claim they wrote a confidential memorandum to Paul Crouch Sr., alleging that 'we think current TBN practices and procedures violate the IRS Code and State and Federal Laws... we do not feel comfortable being

Secretary/Treasurer without bringing these issues forward.'"

Her concerns included the expensive houses, vehicles, and other assets that were used exclusively by Crouch family members but accounted for as ministry expenses. She has been highly critical of the alleged extravagances of her uncle Matthew Crouch, Vice President, and the many millions of dollars he transferred into the film company that he ran.

Brittany was also quoted in the Orange County Register as saying, "But God uses people to different ends, and he's using me to expose this. He doesn't want the money-changers in his house anymore. God is using me to clean house and get TBN into the hands of someone who will ensure it's run properly." She sighed with resignation. "I can handle it. I'm strong. I'm educated. God has provided for us this whole way, I expect he will continue to provide for us."

[From beloved granddaughter to exiled accuser: Brittany Koper and TBN – Orange County Register](#)

Brittany was willing to give up the financial windfall that could have been hers if only she had kept her mouth shut. She could have become a clone of Jan and stayed on at TBN. Most of the robotic children of the rich and famous preachers soon become clones of their parents.

I wonder why anyone would be led to believe that God does not see all of this. You can run, but you can't hide from God, and be sure your sin will find you out. Ouch! Koper said, "TBN, a nonprofit, had sent more than $50 million to Matthew Crouch's for-profit film company for a decade."

It was the expenses charged to Trinity by her uncle Matthew Crouch, her dad's younger brother, that were the last straw. "His lifestyle makes my grandparents' lifestyle look tame," she said. "You can't even compare. My grandfather had a luxury car--but Matt had a new luxury car every other week, and his wife would have one, too. TBN remodeled an entire TBN-owned house for them so that they could have a closet for their designer clothes."

Another interesting story is that of Sylvia Fleener, author of *The Omega Syndrome*. Sylvia had the website, TBN Exposed, where she documented the many abuses of the counterfeit Christian network.

In 2000, Sylvia filed a forty-million-dollar lawsuit against TBN, claiming that *The Omega Code*, the 1999 apocalyptic movie, was originally her story. The case was later settled after a few years of legal wrangling, and the settlement remains confidential.

For more than thirty years, Jackie Alnor has documented the abuses of the apostate church and televangelists. Her book, *The Fleecing of Christianity*, exposes the falling away of the church and TBN's role in this spiritual tragedy.

In 2012, Jackie interviewed Brittany Crouch, and the secrets of TBN were revealed. And it was in this interview that it was alleged by Brittany that Matt Crouch was not the biological son of Paul Crouch but was fathered by muscleman and twin look-alike of Matt Crouch, hunky Mr. America 1954, Dick Dubois. You can find his photos online.

Brittany also states, and I quote: "Ever since I was a little girl, they never lived together ... Grandma had her house and Papa had his house and that's just the way it was."

When the Crouches died, both of their California mansions were sold. This was the story about Paul's mansion.

Quote from the *Orange County Register*, July 21, 2016: "A 'flamboyant' 5,200-square-foot Newport Beach estate once owned by Trinity

Broadcasting Network founder Paul Crouch is for sale at just under $4.6 million."

Why am I saying all this? We are told in the Word to recognize all those who labor among us, especially when they claim to be sheep, but they are wolves!

What is the need for gag orders and confidentiality agreements if you have nothing to hide? Our lives should be an open book, especially if we live them out in public, but these organizations want their employees sworn to secrecy.

Jan Crouch had allowed many false teachers, including Catholic priests, to have airtime on TBN. She was also close to the accused serial molester, the late Earl Paulk, whose heretical teachings Jan loved and promoted.

How could a woman who has been given so much use it for the detriment of the body of Christ? Jan was a pretty lady, yet she made herself look bizarre.

Remember I said a while back that I was going to sell my TV airtime for $50 an hour? Let me give you some calculations here if we had sold twenty hours of airtime a day:

$$20 \times \$50 = \$1,000 \text{ per day}$$
$$\$7,000 \text{ per week}$$

$$\$28,000 \text{ per month}$$
$$12 \text{ months} = \$360,000 \text{ per year}$$

That would have been plenty of money to run our network without doing any fundraising at all.

The airtime on TBN the last time that I heard was about $5,000 an hour. But don't quote me; it could be different now, so here are some potential figures.

$$\$5,000 \text{ an hour} \times 20 \text{ hours} = \$100,000 \text{ per day}$$

$$\$100,000 \text{ a day} \times 7 \text{ days a week} = \$700,000 \text{ weekly}$$

$700,000 a week x 4 weeks
$2,800,000 monthly
For a staggering total in airtime revenue of $33,600,000.00 dollars a year, yes, 33 million

Telethons are not really needed, and asking you to keep TBN on the air with donations does just not sound ethical when it actually sustains itself. They needed the extra money to buy stations and buildings that were rarely used. The money was not just used to preach the gospel. The satellite network all by itself should have been adequate for the preaching of the gospel.

In a recent interview Paul Crouch Jr. stated that TBN took in $100 million in airtime sales and $100 million in donations at one point.

The telethons were gimmicks designed to get you to support the lifestyles of the very rich and famous and to help them buy studios and houses all over the United States and the world that they rarely use. How many live programs were done using the many TBN studios? Not many.

They owned two corporate jets, as reported by Brittany, one for eight million dollars and the other for about fifty million, while you may have been riding a bike or taking a bus.

Many have learned from the Crouches about how to fleece the flock. A terrible legacy to leave behind as they kissed the ring of the Crouches begging for face time.

In addition to greed and false teaching, the Crouches also disregarded God's Word by engaging in ungodly relationships. In the interview, Brittany had this exchange with Jackie Alnor:

J: "What about this Jesus character at the Holyland Experience? I saw them on Behind the Scenes, I watch the show like I said, you don't - and she was doing this whole tour behind the scenes arm-in-arm with this guy, like snuggling with him through this whole thing. It was like shocking how indiscreet it was. Do you have any insight into that?"

B: "Oh, absolutely. Yeah, it was very bizarre to me because when I went over to visit my grandmother in Orlando, he was always around. And they would hold hands and walk together and I witnessed them snuggling, exchanging kisses, and I'm like going, What? What in the world? And I asked her about it. I said, 'Grandma, what are you doing?' And she said, 'Oh, I kiss everybody on the lips.' And I said, 'What?' And she said, 'Yeah, I kiss everybody on the lips. It's not a big deal. It doesn't mean anything.' And it's like, I don't know, it made me very very uncomfortable. I can say that."

Have you ever noticed that people involved in false teachings also have questionable private lives? The works of the flesh become quite obvious because of the compromise.

> *"Now the works of the flesh are manifest, which are these; Adultery, fornication,*

uncleanness, lasciviousness, idolatry, witchcraft, hatred, variance, emulations, wrath, strife, seditions, heresies, envyings, murders, drunkenness, retellings, and such like: of the which I tell you before, as I have also told you in time past, that they which do such things shall not inherit the kingdom of God."
Ephesians 5:19-21

Jan Crouch suffered a massive stroke in May of 2016 and died a few days later without ever seeing Paul Jr. or his family. They did not attend the funeral, and Paul was reportedly denied access to his dying mother.

Matt Crouch now runs the network, along with his wife, Laurie. Gone are the ridiculous telethons and the gaudy sets. Matt owns several properties, and one is a 20,000 sq. ft. mansion in the Colorado Rockies. He paid $10.9 million for the ranch. Paul Crouch Jr. has made several testimonial videos on YouTube, confirming many of the claims in this chapter. Here is a link to one of his testimonies:

[Paul Crouch Jr. Reveals the Truth of His Time at TBN - YouTube](#)

TBN filed numerous lawsuits against Brittany, the once-loved granddaughter. Spending millions in legal fees with what appeared to be unending harassment. This was part of the legacy of the real Jan Crouch.

Chapter 10
Paula White

"Notwithstanding I have a few things against thee, because thou sufferest that woman Jezebel, which calleth herself a prophetess, to teach and to seduce my servants to commit fornication, and to eat things sacrificed unto idols."

Revelation 2:20

Paula White arrived on the gospel scene using deception and financial chicanery. While I was watching television one day, there was Paula and her ex-husband Randy White on the screen. They would come to our local "Christian" Television Network, CTN, in Clearwater, Florida, with large checks, smiling broadly and saying that they were sowing seeds. Or maybe they were trying to buy the favor of the station's president for free airtime. The two regularly used gimmicks to attract attention to themselves.

Paula and Randy started a church in Tampa, and it was called Tampa Christian Center. It later became Without Walls, and it was really without walls when it went bankrupt and was bulldozed years later.

During her first marriage to Dean Knight, Paula opines that she lived in a trailer, which turned out to be a very nice mobile home on a few acres that was built on a solid foundation. For a young married couple just starting, it was a good beginning. She was never "trailer trash," but she claims some people referred to her as that.

Her stepfather was an admiral, so from the age of nine, she enjoyed a very comfortable lifestyle.

It was her choice to live in a mobile home, or trailer as she calls, it at about eighteen. Pregnant and unmarried with her son Brad, she married the baby's father, Harold Dean Knight. Paula says that her father committed suicide when she was five. A newspaper story reported that his car, as it was going around a curve, went off the road while traveling at a high rate of speed, and he was ejected from the car. In those days, people did not wear seat belts.

Paula once made a statement in a video clip that maybe it was not a suicide. Unfortunately, Paula is known for stretching the truth to fit her narrative; maybe it is to gain sympathy from her audience.

Here is the newspaper story that was published at the time of the accident:
Source: *Northeast Mississippi Daily Journal* April 26, 1971

Tupelo Man Killed In 1-Car Accident

A Tupelo man was killed instantly in a one-auto accident at 11:45 a.m. Saturday on Highway 78 east of Holly Springs.

Officers said Donald P. Furr III, 29, apparently lost control of his east-bound vehicle on a curve and went off the right side of the highway just outside Holly Springs city limits near Lake Center Restaurant.

Mississippi Highway Patrolman T. K. Clayton, who investigated the accident, said that according to two or three witnesses the 1968 Plymouth "was traveling at an excessive rate of speed and turned over four or five times."

Patrolman Clayton added that Furr, who was dead on arrival at the Marshall County Hospital, was apparently killed instantly having been thrown out of the over-turning car.

Funeral services were held at 5 p.m. Sunday in the Funeral Chapel at W. E. Pegues with burial in Glenwood Cemetery. The Rev. Garland Holloman officiated.

Furr, co-owner of Playland Toy Stores, lived on Ida Street. A graduate of Tupelo High School, he attended the University of Mississippi. He was a member of the First United Methodist Church and a member of the Tupelo Jaycees.

Pallbearers were Ernie Blackwell, Jimmy Riley, Bobby Edwards, David Hervey, Jimmy Coggins, Dan Ballard, Bill McGuire and Jeff Troyka.

He is survived by a daughter, Paula Michelle and one son, David Mark; his parents, Mr. and Mrs. Donald P. Furr Jr.; a sister, Susan Furr; his grandparents, Mr. and Mrs. Donald P. Furr Sr. and Mrs. John Sims, all of Tupelo. h

---

Tupelo man killed in one car accident

Donald Furr, age 29 Paula's Father

Her life would change radically after she began an affair with the married Randy

White. Both divorced their spouses, and they married in 1990. The marriage lasted about seventeen years. They divorced in 2007.

Here are some examples of the income that the Whites collected over the years. It was obtained from "The Grassley Report" when they were being investigated by the government.

Income was obtained from the Senate report of Senator Grassley

Conferences and Events

$1,519,144.00	2004
$ 1,696,259.00	2005
$ 1,208,597.00	2006

Other Income Total Support and Revenue

$ 21,620,750.00	2004
$ 28,362,192.00	2005
$ 39,933,163.00	2006

Housing Allowances

$713,779.00 $ 883,120.00

EXPENSES

Advertising and Print Media (unknown)

$ 1,230,746.00 $2,031,861.00

Airtime

$ 6,536,246.00
Travel and Transportation
$8,757,318.00
$ 2,417,212.00

Interest and Financing costs

Long-term Debt

$ 13,273,490.00 $22,507,150.00

Airplane Lease

$ 2,659,079.00
$ 1,221,784.00
$2,932,862.00

Through the years, Paula and Randy pulled in over one hundred million dollars, but in 2014, Without Walls filed for bankruptcy. Where did all the money go?

They bought a mansion on Bayshore Blvd. in Tampa, a multi-million-dollar condo at Trump Park Avenue in Manhattan, expensive cars, a jet, and other luxuries.

Also, on the list to benefit from her scams was T.D. Jakes, Daddy to Paula. She often referred to Jakes and his wife Serita as her spiritual parents. She previously was invited to preach at T.D.'s Mega Fest meetings which had been very lucrative for Paula. So, it seems to seal the deal; she bought him or bribed him with a brand-new Bentley, a car that could cost over two hundred thousand dollars. Paula drives in luxury, and so does her "Daddy."

Some of her scams include first fruits and day of atonement offerings (maybe someone forgot to tell Paula that Jesus was the atonement offering).

And then there are Passover scams (and God has passed over Paula), seeds of money to defeat your enemies, and debt cancellation, even though Paula couldn't get her debts canceled. She helped to bankrupt two churches; the Lakeland church was sold at auction, and the Without Walls sold just before the foreclosure auction. They owed the Evangelical Christian Credit Union millions.

Paula flew the coop out of Tampa to the more profitable digs at the New Destiny Christian Center in Apopka, Florida, still reeling from the drug overdose death of their much-loved pastor, Zachary Tims.

She could smell good prey when she saw it, and leaving behind the mess in Tampa and Lakeland for ex-husband Randy to clean up, she weaseled her way into the hearts of the simple at New Destiny, even pushing aside Riva Tims, the ex-wife of Zach and his children.

"Apostle Paula," as she now wants to be called, helped to bankrupt two churches, but she now says she is an apostle. Apostle of what? Apostle of how to fleece people with a Bible by pretending to be a Christian. Don't let that Botox smile fool ya.

Underneath that plastic exterior is someone who has no qualms about putting her head down on her pillow at night, knowing she is a fraud and laughing all the way to the bank by using the precious name of Jesus to get what she wants.

No amount of money moves the hand of God on our behalf, for He has freely given us all things! FREELY!!

The Tampa Tribune published many articles about the rise and fall of Without Walls

International Church, including Camillo Gargano's resignation letter. The church accountant described a church in turmoil and reported, "Handling of finances by upper management is contrary to my fiduciary responsibility."

Management didn't seem bothered by the financial problems, and used "bullying, excessive force and verbal abuse as a management style," Gargano wrote. "Not only is it unconscionable for me to work in such a hostile environment, but it is also physically and mentally debilitating to work under such stressful circumstances." By Baird Helgeson and Michelle Bearden Published: November 6, 2008, Tampa Tribune.

Paula, after her divorce from Randy, and the still-married Benny Hinn were photographed in Rome, Italy, by *The National Enquirer*. 02 Aug 2010. Benny's divorce had been filed but was not finalized when Benny and Paula jetted off to Rome on separate planes, according to Hinn, for a supposed visit to the Vatican.

They were spotted holding hands. Both later denied in statements that were put up on their websites that it was nothing more than a close friendship. It was a major story that put a crunch on Benny's donations.

Later, when Hinn reunited with his wife, Suzanne, she became a Paula White look-a-like, which was kind of bizarre. She had the same hairstyle as Paula, and she dyed her black hair blond.

The saga continued, and the Lakeland, Florida, property was another story. Once an Assembly of God church seating over 9,500 people, the property sat on over sixty-three acres. It later became Without Walls Central. There is also a very large historic building, which was built in the 1920s with over 200 rooms, which once was a retirement home for carpenters.

Apparently, the Whites planned to use it for a school, among many other plans that fell through there.

Finally, they abandoned the properties. The county shut off the power for non-payment of their electric bill for about three years, and the property was finally foreclosed and sold at auction in July 2014.

During about a three-year period, the property was continually vandalized. I went there personally in June 2014 to see the damage.

Hundreds of broken windows, damaged plumbing, and terrible devastation. I was told that the air conditioning systems were vandalized, toilets overflowed, and drywall was torn down. Millions of dollars in destruction. I have video documentation of some of the damage on my YouTube channel, which is under my name and Prophetic News TV.

Yet, the Whites continued to receive salaries, as was documented in the bankruptcy filing,

Randy was paid one hundred fifty thousand dollars a year salary, yet they would not provide permanent security for property worth over ten million. I called Without Walls myself and reported the vandalism in 2011. I also spoke with a real estate agent handling the sale, and he told me the Whites did not have any money for security at the Lakeland site.

According to New York City court records, Paula and Randy had over nine hundred thousand dollars in equity in their Park Avenue condominium, but they were not going to use their own money to save those buildings or pay for security.

They bought it in 2005 from the Trump organization for $3.5 million. In 2019, they paid off the condominium on Park Avenue for $2,625,000. Both their names were on the satisfaction of mortgage, even though they were divorced.

They owed many creditors, including $13.9 million to the credit union, and the property sold for two million at auction, far below what they owed. If you search on the internet, there are videos of abandoned buildings and Without Walls. Lakeland is one of the buildings. A baby grand piano sits gathering mold in one frame as they document the destruction of this once-pristine property.

Why talk about the Whites's financial problems? Because they claimed your financial problems could be solved by tithing 10% of your income and sowing money to them for the ministry, yet they were not able to pay their bills. In 2014, Without Walls settled their debts in bankruptcy court.

The former administration building at the Tampa location, about four stories high that once housed the Paula White television studios and offices, was left derelict.

I visited the property twice; once, I witnessed broken windows, electrical wiring hanging out of the building, and a dirty old mattress sitting by the once-beautiful fountain, a testimony to the judgment of God on the "ministry" of Paula White. On my second visit, I witnessed bulldozers razing the property. Both buildings were demolished in June 2015.

VACATE

BY ORDER OF FIRE CODE ORDINANCE 5072,
ADOPTING NFPA 1 2006 EDITION, CHAPTER 1, SECTION 1.7.14.1,

THIS STRUCTURE IS UNSAFE FOR HUMAN OCCUPANCY AND ORDERED VACATED

THIS STRUCTURE MUST
REMAIN VACANT AND UNOCCUPIED UNTIL
ALL VIOLATIONS ARE CORRECTED.

A PENALTY IS PROVIDED IN THE ORDINANCE STATED ABOVE FOR ANY PERSON WHO ALTERS, DEFACES, OR REMOVES THIS NOTICE OR OCCUPIES THIS DWELLING WITHOUT AUTHORIZATION OF THE FIRE MARSHAL OR DESIGNEE.

DATE PLACARDED: SEPTEMBER 30TH, 2011   PHONE: (863)834-8201
MUST BE VACATED BY: SEPTEMBER 30TH, 2011
                   DATE   FIRE MARSHAL

Sign posted by the county at the Lakeland, Florida: location not safe for human occupancy

Damage at the Lakeland church

Bankruptcy auction at Lakeland, FL
You can go here to see the Tampa bankruptcy filing:

UNITED STATES BANKRUPTCY COURT

https://ia801403.us.archive.org/29/items/gov.uscourts.flmb.1136819/gov.uscourts.flmb.1136819.54.0.pdf

In re: Chapter 11 WITHOUT WALLS INTERNATIONAL CHURCH, INC., Case No. 8:14-bk-2567-MGW 7

Randy met in this building after the fall. He later met in another building not too far from this one in Tampa. Randy later resigned as pastor as he struggled with health problems among other issues. He was cited again in 2023 for DUI.

Paula White, then forty-nine, and Jonathan Cain (Friga), sixty-five, from the rock band Journey, staged a wedding on April 25, 2015, in Orlando, Florida. She had two staged weddings, or three, as she claimed they were first married in Ghana in 2014 by Duncan Williams, then two weddings in April. One for her elite friends with steak and champagne and then cake and punch for the "family" at New Destiny.

Oh, and by the way, neither of the two "marriages" were legal, since they did not get a marriage license until February 2016. I have a copy of the marriage license that I will post here. Her third marriage and his third. He said that he met her on an airplane (he was married at the time) in 2011. He divorced his wife in October of 2014.

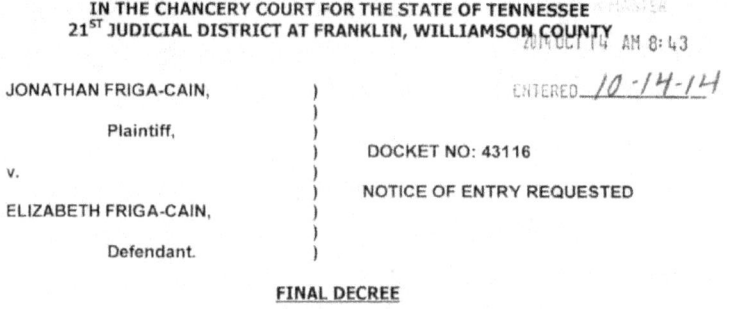

IN THE CHANCERY COURT FOR THE STATE OF TENNESSEE
21ST JUDICIAL DISTRICT AT FRANKLIN, WILLIAMSON COUNTY

2014 OCT 14 AM 8:43

JONATHAN FRIGA-CAIN,

Plaintiff,

v.

ELIZABETH FRIGA-CAIN,

Defendant.

ENTERED 10-14-14

DOCKET NO: 43116

NOTICE OF ENTRY REQUESTED

FINAL DECREE

This cause was heard on the 14th day of October, 2014, before the Honorable Joseph A. Woodruff, Chancery Court Judge of Williamson County, Tennessee, on the

Paula White

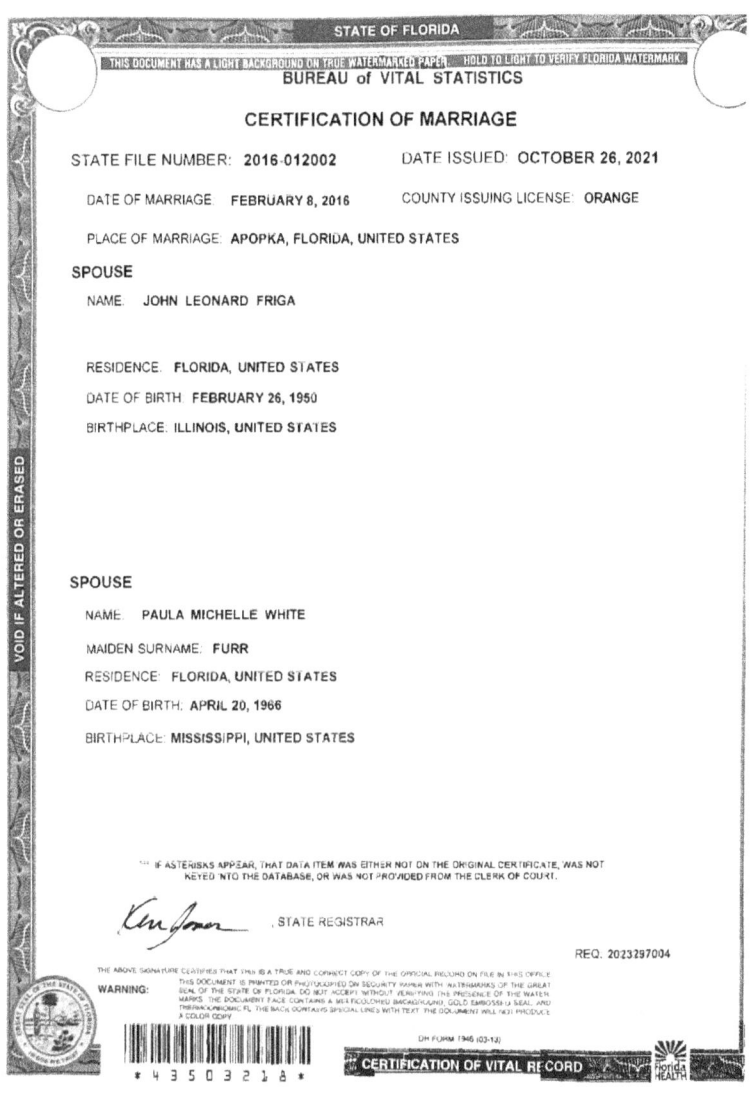

Paula and Jon's marriage license from February 2016 all other marriages were not legal

In 2015, Paula and her new so-called husband Jonathan Cain told the congregation at a Sunday morning service to use porn to spice up their marriages. Jonathan stated if your husband likes porn, watch it with him as Paula giggled in the background.

The room was filled with children, teenagers, and families. Yet this woman was advising a president.

Link to video of Jon saying to use porn.

https://youtu.be/UMbXrL7q1zU?si=WvGiWk2WqPQdwkDp

Her association with Donald Trump has brought Paula national attention. I have written an extensive biography about Paula titled *President Trump's Pastor, Paula White*. It is available on Amazon. Trump uses her as his "spiritual advisor," and that is not saying much about his lack of judgment when it comes to Paula.

The two of them have shared a platform with the notorious cult leader and wife of the late Sun Myung Moon. Both speak at Mrs.

Moon's conferences, and they praise her as a tremendous person.

Paula, in her delusion, said that Mrs. Moon loves the Lord and that she is a Christian. Mr. Moon claimed to be the Messiah, and his wife now claims to be the Holy Spirit and the only begotten daughter of God. They say Jesus was a failure and that they must finish the job of bringing salvation to the world.

Trump and Paula received large sums of money for their appearances. Trump has reportedly received millions, as it was reported in the *Washington Post*, from Moon. Christians, beware of false prophets, for they practice to deceive.

Chapter 11

Juanita Bynum

"Lying lips are abomination to the LORD: but they that deal truly are his delight."

Proverbs 12:22

Most of the time when you see Juanita, it looks like she is wearing a tent; it is that huge white gown with blue stripes. She also has an array of strange costumes that she wears to do her act, and it is an act.

We did not see much of her for a while on TV, but then the "Word Network," or "Un-Word Network" as I like to call it, featured her doing their beg-a-thons, trinket selling, and whatever else they can pay her to do to help them raise funds to keep the sheep fleecing operation on the air.

She also lays prostrate on "prayer shawls" in a foolish display so that you then can be the beneficiary of one of these "anointed" shawls for an offering.

Her incessant screaming borders on total insanity. I wonder how many microphones she has blown out?

Juanita appeared on the scene when T.D. Jakes had her as a speaker at Mega Fest, with her "no more sheets" story. Married for a brief time in a reported million-dollar wedding ceremony to Thomas Weeks, the marriage fell apart when Juanita accused Tommy of beating her in a highly publicized divorce battle.

In 2008, after initially pleading not guilty to charges of aggravated assault and making terroristic threats, Weeks pleaded guilty to a single count of aggravated assault, admitting that he grabbed Bynum, threw her down, and kicked her. Weeks was sentenced to three years' probation. They divorced in June 2008.

Thomas found a new honey and dropped Juanita without looking back. So much for love.

He was seen afterward running his own seed-sowing operation, or how to make the preacher rich, by giving money to God.

When televangelists lose credibility, they often use advertising techniques to rebrand themselves. Juanita promoted herself as Ambassador, Doctor Bynum, and even wanted the title of Bishop.

While preaching at Rod Parsley's church, in 2002 at Dominion Camp meeting Juanita made the following comments. She warns the "dumb sheep," as she called them that day, not to question the pastor, much to the delight of Rod Parsley. Do not correct the "Mand of Gawd." Wow! She was telling the people they were not smart enough to question the pastor.

"She said she don't care what God is leading you to do; if He didn't tell your 'pastor,' you can't go.

"God ain't never told you to check your pastor." So, if Rod Parsley becomes a cult leader, don't question him? Ridiculous. https://www.youtube.com/watch?v=ktP581tT0Rg&list=PLR4FSCuQeJms9e_5DzvDZxkvRg_8VjCfD

Apostlette Veter Nichols is a spiritual mother and mentor to Juanita Bynum. In a YouTube video, Veter said the fake apostle, David E. Taylor, saw Jesus, and their Jesus gave him the keys to the kingdom. Veter claims that she disobeyed prophet Taylor and almost died, but she then sowed $5,000, obeyed the "prophet," and received her inheritance of eighty million dollars. Juanita seems to mimic her spiritual mother. Like mother, like daughter, they say. Now Juanita has photos of Jesus supposedly coming to her services. But trust me, Jesus was nowhere near that mess. We do not use images of the Lord

Jesus. It is forbidden. I do not believe any testimony of people saying that they see Jesus, that they have heavenly visitations, or that Jesus is talking with them audibly. Jesus is sitting at the right hand of the Father. He will return, but He certainly did not return for Juanita.

She had a working relationship with Catholic Michelle Corral, who masquerades as an Evangelical Christian. I saw Michelle on the Benny Hinn program years ago with two Catholic priests. She spoke about her Catholic faith. She is known to associate with other spooky, way-out-there preachers just like herself. Because of the deception that she walks in; she attracts false teachers and false prophets.

In 2009, a birthday bash was held for her fiftieth birthday. The cost was $200 to attend. That was some lucrative party. She made out like the bandit that she is.

A few years ago, Bynum started "The Lotus Foundation," and in the literature for the foundation, she explains the meaning of the lotus flower.

Lotus flower symbolism (from Juanita's website, The Lotus foundation): "The Lotus is a plant that belongs to the *Nelumbo* genus, and it has long been associated with purity, rebirth, and divinity."

Some, but not all, of the lotus flower symbolism is different across the major cultures in that it plays a role. For instance, in Buddhism, it is seen as a sign of purity, associated with beauty in Hinduism, and with the sun in Egyptology; more recently, the significance of the lotus has been incorporated into the Bahai religion.

A thing that is striking about the lotus is that although it often grows in mud, and returns within it at night, it always flowers clean the following day; this makes it a great item for a metaphor. It also led the great Chinese philosopher Confucius to state, "I have a love for the lotus, while growing in mud still remains unstained." She also quotes Mahatma Gandhi, as her New Age leanings are coming to light; what she once tried to hide is no longer hidden.

Juanita is now holding prayer schools at $1500 a clip. This is a quote from Bynum, who was highly criticized for her actions. Quote from the *Christian Post*: September 20th 2022.
"This is not some cheap-based class where we're going to be in there swinging from chandeliers and giving you two tots about some Scripture in the Bible and we're going to call that a school of prayer."

Juanita's Mugshot

"Popular televangelist Juanita Bynum was arrested and spent the night in jail on a warrant charging that she failed to appear in court for a civil proceeding against her. https://www.dallasnews.com/news/crime/2013/04/19/televangelist-juanita-bynum-jailed-in-dallas-for-failure-to-appear-in-civil-proceeding/

Chapter 12

Marilyn Hickey

"If ye fulfil the royal law according to the scripture, Thou shalt love thy neighbour as thyself, ye do well:"

James 2:8

Marilyn can quote the Word. She is a very bright and energetic Bible teacher. The first time I encountered Marilyn was on Christian radio after I was born again in 1981.

I so enjoyed her Bible studies, and I made it a point to drive over to Denver just to hear her since I was living in Colorado at the time. Her church was called "Happy Church," and it was a happy place. Marilyn and her quirky husband Wally seemed like polar opposites.

I did not have much personal contact with Marilyn, although I was invited by the singles pastor to be the guest speaker at their annual singles conference.

I was thrilled with the invitation, and we spent the weekend at a resort in Silverthorne, Colorado. Over the years, I traveled to Happy Church at least two more times to minister to the singles.

Over the years, I lost contact with Happy Church. Marilyn and Wally later appeared in the audience at Carpenters Home Church in Lakeland, Florida, at a Rodney-Howard Browne service, which I also attended. Many famous people were there, receiving drinks from the "Holy Ghost bartender," as Rodney called himself. The deception was great, and many of us bought into it. Rodney was a master manipulator.

He prophesied many great things for the future of Carpenters Home Church and Karl Strader, but none of them came to pass. The over 9,000-seat sanctuary is no longer standing. Sadly, it has been demolished. So much for Rodney's false prophecies.

One time I called her prayer line for prayer, and they would not pray for me until I signed up for the mailing list. I wanted prayer. I did not want to be solicited for donations.

This is when I began to realize some ministries used their prayer lines not just for prayer, but for soliciting funds. This grieved me, and I am sure others felt the same way.

Marilyn at one time was sending out chopsticks, among other trinkets, cornmeal, oil, and other point-of-contact items and they are all used to entice you to return it for a blessing. The con here is that you have to send for something so that they can get your address and then to bombard you with appeal letters. Shameful tactics from a woman who can recite whole chapters of the Bible.

Marilyn served on the board of regents of Oral Roberts University and was also on the board for Pastor Paul Yonggi Cho of South Korea, who was a convicted criminal. He passed away in 2021.

On February 26, 2014, *The Buffington Post* reported:

"David Yonggi Cho, founder of South Korea's Yoido Full Gospel Church, has been sentenced to three years in prison for embezzling $12 million in church funds, Christianity Today reported on Monday.

Allegations arose in November of last year when 30 church elders held a press conference accusing Cho and his family of stealing millions in church donations dating back to the 1990s. The elders enumerated multiple instances of Cho's dishonesty that involved him borrowing and never returning funds, acquiring enormous church donations without disclosing what they were being used toward and even taking an $18 million severance pay when he stepped down as head pastor in 2008.

"On February 21, the Seoul Central Court found Cho guilty of embezzlement from encouraging church officials in 2002 to buy stock owned by his son at four times the market value, according to Yonhap News Agency. In addition to spending three years in prison, Cho will pay $4.6 million in fines as part of his sentence, though if the church elders were right this is still just a fraction of the total funds he stole."

Greed never ends well, from opulent riches to prison orange.

A few years ago, Marilyn had a nervous breakdown. I believe God was trying to get her attention as she spoke about it on television. Her husband, Wally, was ill with dementia, and he later died. This would have been a good time for her to examine herself and to get things right with God. But instead, it was business as usual. Even appearing with Benny Hinn as she promised the seed sower's miracles if they would send money.

Her daughter, Sarah Bowling, is now her partner, and Sarah's husband, Reece, pastors the church. Sarah just goes along with the family business and never seems to break out on her own with anything else except what she learned from Mom.

Born in 1931, Marilyn is now ninety-three. Can she change? It is never too late! As Jesus said to Lazarus, "Marilyn, come forth."

Chapter 13

Kenneth and Gloria Copeland

"But though we, or an angel from heaven, preach any other gospel unto you than that which we have preached unto you, let him be accursed."
Galatians 1:8

Kenneth and Gloria Copeland enjoy a life of unprecedented wealth as charismatic preachers. Once a pilot and chauffeur for Oral Roberts, Kenneth somehow managed to work his way up the ladder of tremendous success in ministry.

They have been playing some of his older programs recently, some from over twenty years ago, and he is just so arrogant and puffed up with pride as ever. How did I ever listen to this man?

Their books on prosperity were in my library, and I was drawn into their teachings by the promises of giving to get, especially the hundred-fold return. I thought it was for unselfish reasons, but, of course, it was selfishness. I thought that God required it, the giving to get.

I attended a few of their believers' conventions, and at that time, a full band traveled with him made up of very talented singers and musicians. And Kenneth, he could prophesy. He also fancied himself a prophet.

Kenneth is a singer, and he would perform his solos, and then came the preaching. He was a "Word" man, even though he said strange things, like Jesus had to be born again, and Jesus went to hell and had to fight the devil. Now that was a good piece of fiction right there.

After all, he was a friend of the Hagins and the Roberts; he sure could drop names. He had men like Jesse Duplantis, Jerry Savelle, and Norvel Hayes teaching at the meetings.

And, of course, there was Gloria and her healing school. I remember that she held her school in the afternoons. She wore the most beautiful dresses, and back then, the women preachers were dressed to the hilt. I still like to see women in dresses when they preach; it looks so much more feminine.

Gloria would go over the healing scriptures, and then they would have a prayer line. I believe that Jesus is a healer and that He still performs miracles. I do not believe it happens because some so-called great one lays hands on you. And I do believe in the laying on of hands. If people received healing, it wasn't because of Gloria.

Kellie and John are the Copelands' children. Kellie has had three husbands, and Kenneth has other children from a previous marriage or two.

The Copelands are big on talking about love, but they do not always practice what they preach when it comes to someone challenging them about their error. The fangs will come out!

Kenneth can get downright nasty. When a TV reporter confronted him about his wealth, with a scowl on his face, he said, "None yo' business."

Here is some information from Wikipedia:

"Kenneth Copeland Ministries is located at 14355 Morris Dido Road, Fort Worth, TX 76192 on 33 acres and was valued at $554,160 in 2008 by Tarrant Appraisal District.

"The site includes the Eagle Mountain International Church, television production and audio recording facilities, warehouse and distribution facilities, residences for the Copeland family, and Kenneth Copeland Airport. Approximately 500 people are employed by KCM.

"KCM also owns a 1998 Cessna 550 Citation Bravo, which it received from a donor in October 2007 and is used for domestic flights, and a 2005 Cessna 750 Citation X, which it uses for international flights. It also is restoring a 1962 Beech H-18 Twin, which the ministry plans to use for disaster relief efforts.

"Kenneth and Gloria also own a huge 18,000-square-foot house and it is reportedly worth over 6 million dollars. Those hundredfold blessings sure worked for them."

Ken came out of the ecumenical closet by recently meeting with fellow wolf supreme "Pope Francis" at the Vatican of all places.

His liaison was the late Tony Palmer, recently killed in a head-on crash on his motorcycle, who masqueraded as an Evangelical Christian. However, I believe he was a Catholic, especially since his funeral in Bath, England, was held in a Catholic cathedral and was a high requiem Mass. He was also buried in a Catholic cemetery.

Being a former Catholic myself, I attended Catholic school for seven years in the late 1950s and early 60s. I know how things work or how they are supposed to work, as I was heavily indoctrinated into the Catechism, not ever in the Bible. We never opened it! We were told not to read it, because we would not understand it, and we needed the priest to interpret it.

Palmer worked for Copeland at his office in South Africa about twenty years ago. It has been said by former Jesuits that they infiltrate organizations to help bring all people back to the Holy Mother Church. So, I suspect that it is no coincidence that the new pope is a Jesuit, and he is arranging meetings at the Vatican with other Kool-Aid drinkers such as James Robison and John Arnott.

Palmer appeared at a recent Kenneth Copeland ministers' conference, spewing his false doctrine to the gullible blind sheep who were present. Palmer tried to persuade his charismatic audience to end their opposition to dangerous Catholic theology.

Here are some quotes from Palmer at the Copeland ministers' conference in 2014:
"'The Catholic and Charismatic Renewal is the hope of the Church,' exclaims Anglican Episcopal Bishop Tony Palmer, before a group of cheering followers at the Kenneth Copeland Ministries. Palmer said those words were from the Vatican. Before playing the video message from Pope Francis to Kenneth Copeland, Palmer told the crowd, 'When my wife saw that she could be Catholic, and Charismatic, and Evangelical, and Pentecostal, and it was absolutely accepted in the Catholic Church, she said that she would like to reconnect her roots with the Catholic culture. So she did.'

"The crowd cheered, as he continued, 'Brothers and sisters, Luther's protest is over. Is yours?'"

He said the protest was over, but my protest will never be over. First of all, I am a Christian, not a "Protestant." The Catholic church would have you believe that they were the only church before Luther protested, yet history does not bear this out.

But God always had a people. The Catholic war machine has a way of rewriting history.

The Catholic "church" has killed many Bible-believing Christians throughout the centuries; the bloodbath was called the Inquisition, which for years they denied, and thank God for the blessed historians who documented the horrors, such as John Foxe, in his great classic, *Foxe's Book of Martyrs*, first published in 1563, and the masterpiece by J.H. Merle D'Aubigne, D.D., *History of the Reformation of the Sixteenth Century*. (Below is the rack at the Tower of London, instruments of torture room.)

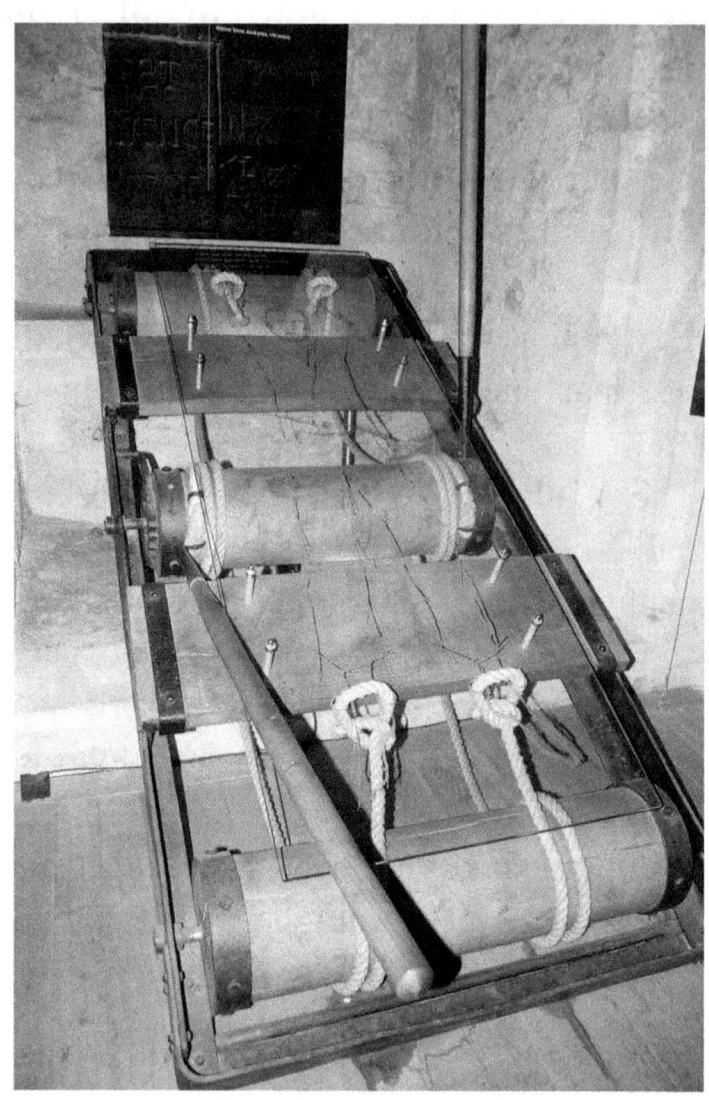

Tyndale and Wycliffe were hunted for their crimes of translating and publishing Bibles for all to read. The Catholic church did not want people reading the Bible, oh, no. Yes, it truly was the Dark Ages.

You can see some of the remnants of the Inquisition at the Tower of London in London, England, as I did when I visited the tower. There they have a special room set aside called the instrument of torture room, where the rack is displayed. This extremely brutal form of torture was used on Bible-believing Christians by the wicked popes. It stretched out people's limbs, hoping for a confession to the so-called true church, the mother of all harlots, the Roman Catholic church.

If one did not confess and recant their belief in true biblical Christianity, they were stretched until they died. They were also burned at the stake, as was the fate of William Tyndale.

The Miracle Sellers

"Tyndale was betrayed by Henry Phillips to the imperial authorities, seized in Antwerp in 1535, and held in the castle of Vilvoorde (Filford) near Brussels. He was tried on a charge of heresy in 1536 and condemned to be burned to death, despite Thomas's intercession on his Cromwell's behalf.

"Tyndale 'was strangled to death while tied at the stake, and then his dead body was burned.' His final words, spoken 'at the stake with a fervent zeal, and a loud voice,' were reported as 'Lord! Open the King of England's eyes.'" -From Wikipedia https://en.wikipedia.org/wiki/William_Tyndale

It was a crime at the time to own an English Bible. Greek New Testament was available in Europe, and by Martin Luther. While a number of partial and incomplete translations had been made from the seventh century onward, the grassroots spread of Wycliffe's Bible resulted in a death sentence for any unlicensed possession of Scripture in English

- even though translations in all other major European languages had been accomplished and made available.

Why would a so-called "church" fight so vehemently to stop the publication of the Bible in English? Have nothing, and I mean nothing, to do with this unfruitful work of darkness.

Francis, that was what he renamed himself, but his real name is Jorge, he smiles and says we should forget the past and have a group hug.

Pa---leese--- Spare me, especially as I would have received a death sentence for owning an English Bible from the Catholic church.
And Copeland jumps with glee at this, and the audience erupts in applause. Oh, foolish Galatians, who has bewitched you? (Galatians 3:1)

Does this scene remind you of people taking 666 on their foreheads and aligning with the false prophet and the Antichrist?

"For by thy words, thou shalt be justified, and by thy words thou shalt be condemned."
Matthew 12:37

Some famous Copeland quotes (taken from http://www.forgottenword.org):

"He [Jesus] allowed the devil to drag Him into the depths of hell...He allowed Himself to come under Satan's control...every demon in hell came down on Him to annihilate Him...They tortured Him beyond anything anybody had ever conceived. For three days He suffered everything there is to suffer." (Kenneth Copeland, *The Price of It All*, p. 3)

"Jesus went into hell to free mankind from the penalty of Adam's high treason...When His blood poured out it did not atone. Jesus spent three horrible days and nights in the bowels of this earth getting back for you and me our rights with God." (personal letter from Ken Copeland, Ft. Worth, Texas, March 12, 1979., D.R. McConnell, *A Different Gospel*, p. 118)

"I've had ugly books written about me because I said that Jesus died spiritually, but the fact is, I didn't say that the Bible said it. Jesus became our substitute. If he hadn't died spiritually, then we could never have been made alive spiritually. But He did! On the cross, Jesus was separated from the glory of God. He allowed Himself to be made sin for us, and He became obedient to death. He went into the pit of hell and suffered there as though He was the One Who had committed the sin." (Ken Copeland, *The Power of His Resurrection*)

Here are some quotes from "Pope" Francis at the Copeland conference:

"Families that come together and families who separate themselves. We are kind of ... permit me to say, separated.

"Separated because, it's sin that has separated us, all our sins. The misunderstandings throughout history. It has been a long road of sins that we all shared in. Who is to blame? We all share the blame. We have all sinned. There is only one blameless, the Lord. I am nostalgic (yearning), that this separation comes to an end and gives us communion."

The Council of Trent held the Catholic church's position then, and now, it has not changed. "If anyone saith, that by faith alone the impious is justified; in such wise as to mean, that nothing else is required to co-operate in order to the obtaining the grace of Justification, and that it is not in any way necessary, that he be prepared and disposed of by the movement of his own will; let him be anathema."

They say there is no salvation outside of the "holy Mother Church." We say by faith alone we are saved by grace, through faith in our blessed Lord and Savior, Jesus Christ.

We are not part of His family. Only those who have been born again are a part of the family of God. Do we all share the blame for the Inquisition?

Catholic website http://www.catholicism.org explains what they really believe. "Outside the Church there is no salvation" (*extra ecclesiam nulla salus*) is a doctrine of the Catholic Faith that was taught By Jesus Christ to His Apostles, preached by the Fathers, defined by popes and councils and piously believed by the faithful in every age of the Church."
Here is how the Popes defined it:

"There is but one universal Church of the faithful, outside which no one at all is saved." (Pope Innocent III, Fourth Lateran Council, 1215)

"We declare, say, define, and pronounce that it is absolutely necessary for the salvation of every human creature to be subject to the

Roman Pontiff." (Pope Boniface VIII, the Bull Unam Sanctam, 1302)

"The most Holy Roman Church firmly believes, professes and preaches that none of those existing outside the Catholic Church, not only pagans, but also Jews and heretics and schismatics, can have a share in life eternal; but that they will go into the eternal fire which was prepared for the devil and his angels, unless before death they are joined with Her; and that so important is the unity of this ecclesiastical body that only those remaining within this unity can profit by the sacraments of the Church unto salvation, and they alone can receive an eternal recompense for their fasts, their alms giving's, their other works of Christian piety and the duties of a Christian soldier. No one, let his alms giving be as great as it may, no one, even if he pour out his blood for the Name of Christ, can be saved, unless he remain within the bosom and the unity of the Catholic Church." (Pope Eugene IV, the Bull Cantate Domino, 1441)

Where did Jesus Christ Himself ever say that there is no salvation outside of the Catholic church?

He said we must come to Him by faith; through grace we are saved and not by joining any organization, because the body of Christ is the church.

Romans 3:24
"Being justified freely by his grace through the redemption that is in Christ Jesus."

Romans 5:2
"By whom also we have access by faith into this grace wherein we stand, and rejoice in hope of the glory of God."

Ephesians 1:7
"In whom we have redemption through his blood, the forgiveness of sins, according to the riches of his grace;"

Ephesians 2:8

"For by grace are ye saved through faith; and that not of yourselves: it is the gift of God."

Quote from "Jorge," Pope Francis, 2013:
"But the Christian identity is not an identity card: Christian identity is belonging to the Church, because all of these belonged to the Church, the Mother Church. Because it is not possible to find Jesus outside the Church. The great Paul VI said: 'Wanting to live with Jesus without the Church, following Jesus outside of the Church, loving Jesus without the Church is an absurd dichotomy.'"

Copeland would have you believe that somehow, we are to unify with this false religious system and that we have common ground. Yet, what is common about believing that Jesus Christ comes down from heaven and lives in a wafer for people to eat? This is a form of mindlessness in my view, yet over one billion people are said to believe it.

Yet, this diabolical institution has managed to convince people that this is true. It points to another Jesus and another gospel.

Beware of the Copelands. Run for your life from them and the others that are drunk with pride. James Robison and John Arnott also made the pilgrimage to Rome to bow the knee and kiss the ring!

The Bible says we are to reject the heretic after the second admonition, not hug and kiss them.

Kenneth now owns a twenty-four-hour television network, The Victory Channel. He recently confessed to getting a pacemaker and that Gloria was having memory problems. She is no longer seen in public. His son, John, confessed in a recent interview with his sister, Kellie herself divorced three times, that he struggled with alcoholism. He now runs a treatment center to rehabilitate people with addiction problems. His wealth has also increased through major payments to his oil and gas leases, tens of millions of dollars. The great man of faith holds telethons, promising miracles to those who sow financial seeds using a cast of characters from his network who then donate millions to the already very rich Copelands.

Chapter 14
Steve Munsey

"For they that are such serve not our Lord Jesus Christ, but their own belly; and by good words and fair speeches deceive the hearts of the simple."

Romans 16:18

Scripture twister extraordinaire! Munsey knew a good gig when he found it becoming a professional fundraiser and using Jesus Christ to do it.

His antics have made him famous in heretic circles. He became a frequent guest on the "Christian," and I use that word loosely, television programs that hire him for his masterful manipulation of the simple-minded sheep yearning for some easy money.

"For the turning away of the simple shall slay them, and the prosperity of fools shall destroy them."
Proverbs 1:32

Who is Steve Munsey? You may have seen him, the guy with the funny blond hair and plastic surgery gone awry. One of his favorite sayings is "Aw, God is fixin'."

Yes, Steve can predict when God will work a miracle, and it always seems to come with a payoff. He is very creative and hears the voice of his master, the devil, as he invents all sorts of schemes to extract your hard-earned cash from your wallet into his and the wallets of the greedy puppet masters who he serves.

"Yea, they are greedy dogs which can never have enough, and they are shepherds that cannot understand: they all look to their own way, every one for his gain."
Isaiah 56:11

Here is an excerpt from a story on titled "Empty Suit Preacher Sinks Illinois Church" https://www.salon.com/2013/03/05/indiana_mega_church_faces_foreclosure_partner/

"As it turns out, the story is about Munsey's church, Family Christian Center, which then claimed to have a weekly attendance of 15,000, making it one of the largest churches in the country.

"According to an investigation by the NWITimes.com, a paper covering northwestern Indiana, the judge presiding over the foreclosure proceedings told attorneys in court, 'When I saw some of the expenditures being made in this church when there was a mortgage not being paid, I was astounded.'

"NWITimes reports that even as the church owed close to $100,000 a month in mortgage payments (not to mention mortgage payments on condos the church claimed to use for visiting clergy, and other unspecified bills in excess of half a million dollars), Munsey and his wife Melodye raked in '$2.9 million in total compensation from 2008 through 2011 from organizations connected to Family Christian Center, IRS records show.'

"In all, 'The church annually spent $3.5 million in leadership compensation and had a $900,000 budget for travel and meals, a $500,000 housing allowance and $500,000 for jet fuel and other expenditures according to the transcript. In 2010 the church paid $1 million for property in Illinois,' the transcript states. 'There's more: an IRS investigation and tax liens, for starters.'

"You can read the whole investigative story, for which Munsey declined to be interviewed."

Obviously, Munsey declined to be interviewed. The product he is trying to sell to you is defective. It is a misrepresentation of the real Jesus.

Again, the pyramid scheme benefits the one on top with the Munsey's hiding behind the facade of prosperity or "look at all we have, and if you do what we tell you, you can have it too."

"Munsey Sinks His Own Church in His Quest for Filthy Lucre (from the http://www.nwi.com, Feb. 17, 2013):

"At the time the mortgage foreclosure case started in 2011, Family Christian Center had been bringing in about $10 million per year and had a $98,000 monthly mortgage payment, a transcript of the Dec. 4, 2012, hearing states."

The Munsey's had not repaid the loan from Refuge Productions as of 2011, IRS records show.

Refuge Productions also owned a Mercedes that cost $80,611 and was part-owner of an airplane that cost the nonprofit more than $100,000 per year in 2007 and 2009, IRS records show. The airplane was not clearly listed in records from 2008, 2010, or 2011.

The Munseys' son, Kent, made at least $914,886 in salary and benefits from 2008 through 2010 from Refuge, Family Christian Center, and City Church Fellowship, IRS records show. City Church Fellowship operates City Church Chicago, which is led by Kent Munsey and his wife Alli. The couple also work at Family Christian Center.

Wow, the son and his family were living large on those tithes and offerings from the debt-ridden congregation.
With the church going under, the Munsey's buy a house for over two million!!

"The same year they took out a $2.3 million dollar mortgage on their home in Briar Ridge subdivision in Schererville.

"The home, which has been put up for sale, has an assessed value of $550,800, according to the Lake County assessor's office."
https://texags.com/forums/15/topics/2278157

Munsey also owns a beachfront condo worth at least two million dollars in Hollywood, Florida.

Munsey, he is the king of all the feast day scammers. He has more phony teachings on supposed feast day blessings than anyone I have ever heard teach on the subject. He can spin a tall tale about how his God has to be appeased on certain "holy" days of the year with money, and only money will force his God to obey the commands of the giver.

Here are some famous or infamous Munsey quotes from telethons and sermons.
"Go to the phone, dial the number on the screen as fast as you can. Give $50 dollars a month for 10 months, God will do a now miracle...Wooo! I feel the Holy Spirit...We

are not talking hocus pocus, this is a word from God...l have come to Dallas and Daystar with a word from God...God is speaking to people to give $5,000."
https://www.azquotes.com/quote/1450704

"The Spirit is speaking strongly to me for you to place a $50 offering on the altar, when you do, God will do a now miracle."

"I'm thinking about cash for you, that's the deal. I've got cash on my mind cause it's getting ready to happen to somebody."
https://preachersaidwhat.wordpress.com/2011/07/27/steve-munsey-said-what/

"And shall receive the reward of unrighteousness, as they that count it pleasure to riot in the day time. Spots they are and blemishes, sporting themselves with their own deceivings while they feast with you;"
2 Peter 2:13

Recently, Steve has hooked up with Rod Parsley as they push the Day of Atonement Feast day, or God's most holy day. I didn't know God had any holy days.

"Your new moons and your appointed feasts my soul hateth: they are a trouble unto me; I am weary to bear them."
Isaiah 1:14

They are very creative as they use our precious Savior for their own gain. Do they not fear God?

When you see Steve Munsey on the TV screen, turn him off and tune him out.

Chapter 15
Todd Coontz

"The prophets prophesy falsely, and the priests bear rule by their means; and my people love to have it so: and what will ye do in the end thereof?"

Jeremiah 5:31

If ever anyone had acted like a used car salesman, it is Todd Coontz. Slick Todd appeared on TV with his seductive commercials, peddling his wares to a desperate audience.

I wondered when I first started seeing him on TV how anyone could take him seriously.

Especially the so-called Bible teachers, which he is not! When it comes to the Bible, he is illiterate.

He was regularly seen with Benny Hinn, Rod Parsley, and many others as they hired Todd to sell the gospel, and he is a hypnotizer in chief. A man who does not act like a born-again Christian and only uses the Bible as a prop. He teaches nothing but empty words, not the true gospel.

Your seed can buy you favor; sounds like something the local psychic fortune teller might tell you.

Jim Bradley of Eyewitness News in Charlotte, North Carolina, reported that Todd lived in a $1.38 million dollar condo and that he drove such luxury cars as Ferrari, Maserati, and BMW.

He did an investigation into Todd's "ministry," which was broadcast on the nightly news, but it was not enough to stop people from sending him money.

Todd says you must act within a specific timeframe; otherwise, his God will pass you by. He snaps his fingers just like all good hypnotists do, and he also uses a form of numerology. This is a tactic many of the false psychic teachers use. When you hear finger snapping, beware.

And, oh yes, you can get a double portion miracle too. He has learned the art of the con from some very good teachers. If it didn't work, he would have another job, and he would not be able to afford the very expensive TV airtime. It is very unfortunate for all the people who have sent Todd money, as none of his promises will ever come to pass.

"But if ye will not do so, behold, ye have sinned against the Lord: and be sure your sin will find you out."
Numbers 32:23

Todd goes to prison:
"Televangelist Todd Coontz has lost the final appeal of his 2019 conviction on tax evasion charges and begun serving a five-year sentence at a Florida prison.

"The U.S. Attorney's Office in the Western District of North Carolina found Coontz guilty in January 2019 of tax fraud and evasion for hiding $1.7 million in income and assets from the government while living a lavish lifestyle, The Charlotte Observer reported. He was released from prison in June of 2024. Did he learn his lesson and will he stop scamming, we shall see."

This was posted on his X page, where he has over 8,000 followers

Dr. Todd Coontz is a Kingdom of God ambassador teaching to nations!

"See, I have this day set thee over the nations and over the kingdoms, to root out, and to pull down, and to destroy, and to throw down, to build, and to plant."

Todd Coontz

Jeremiah 1:10

Chapter 16

God TV

"But whoso committeth adultery with a woman lacketh understanding: he that doeth it destroyeth his own soul."

Proverbs 6:32

Rory Alec (not his real last name) resigned from his position as head of the network because of adultery, which they have coined "moral failure" in 2014.

On October 8, 2014, Wendy Alec gave a full report of what has happened to Rory. Wendy said this had been going on since March, as Rory was mostly absent from her life and the life of the network.

He does not want to be married to her and wants nothing to do with the ministry. His girlfriend was Carola Caye, now his wife;

they married in 2017. Wendy named her "Jezebel" on the broadcast, and they say they are supposed to be together. Wendy and Rory were married for twenty-seven years.

I personally have had friends who had similar experiences, and some of them divorced their wives and married the other woman, saying it was God. Not much of a testimony to a lost and dying world and their children.

Hopefully, this man will get truly saved before it is too late. God does not break up marriages. Evidently, he did not believe anything he was saying, and it was all an act. As for Wendy, this was very painful for her. She had surgery during the separation, and Rory all but abandoned her even then.

False doctrine and false teaching usually go hand in hand with a "moral failure." If you cannot have integrity in the financial area of your ministry, you will not have morals in any other area.

Wendy and Rory also used all the professional "gospel" fundraisers we so often see on television. We hear the same empty false promises over and over again.

There is "Pastor" Benny Hinn, and just what church is he currently "pastoring"? Steve Munsey, Mike Murdock, and Todd Bentley.

The Alecs supported and televised on the God TV network his "revival" meetings that were held in Florida a few years back. Todd kicked people during his services, and his appearance became more bizarre as time went on, adding more tattoos and earrings in his chin and other odd places. Wildly spinning his false doctrines and he even claimed to raise the dead.

Todd also committed adultery and left his wife and children behind for a new wife.

Wendy and Rory would build an altar during telethons where they would put your prayer requests on it after they have manipulated you every way coming and going. Asking you to send a gift to God (them) and then they would try to get you to believe that your money and their prayers will get you an audience with God and special favor.

They used any means without conscience to get you to give, so God can bless you, except the only ones getting "blessed" were them, as they bought multi-million-dollar homes and whatever else their greedy hearts desired. And just maybe spending donations on affairs.

They started God TV in 1995 in Europe. Wendy was born in Britain, and Rory is from South Africa. It started to fill a void since there was not a full-time Christian TV network in Europe at the time.

One of the homes once owned by the Alecs in Kansas:

They were building a ministry center in Plymouth, England, in an old theater, they said for revivals, which they needed themselves. It was said to cost upwards of ten million dollars. Construction work on this project was halted since all this divorce mess. I doubt seriously these two are born again. Their morals are quite suspect, and the fundraising techniques were an abomination.

Repent or go away, Rory and Wendy, and your Un-God TV. (As of this writing, neither

Wendy nor Rory are a part of God TV.) A friend of mine said they have a sign that says one billion souls, but they should include themselves in this campaign.

Here is an infamous quote from Wendy. She said twice that Jesus would visit in person and that Jesus would set His foot upon the stage in a divine, personal, one-to-one visitation.

"GOD TV faces one of the biggest financial challenges the ministry has experienced. We need $1.5 million by 23 May and another $2.5 million in the bank by 31 May. This means a total of $4 million, to enable us to continue broadcasting from Jerusalem to the nations!"

We will see what the future holds for God TV if they will survive this judgment. God may remove them from public ministry as their finances dry up.

Maybe Wendy will sell out to God and let God make something beautiful out of her life. Trying to use Jesus and the precious gospel for your own gain will only end in heartache and trouble.

That's one reason why we sound the alarm with books like this, and along with the other apologetics ministries, maybe our voices can prevent these types of devastating crashes and tragedies.

Wendy Alec has a very low profile these days, as she is no longer seen on God TV. Rory lives with his wife in Europe and has a YouTube channel. A far cry from their former glory days. How the mighty have fallen.

God TV is now Angel Christian Television with offices in Plymouth, England, and Orlando, Florida. The CEO is Ward Simpson.

According to their 990 filing in 2023, their total income for 2023 was just over $6.5 million here in the United States.

Wendy Alec receives compensation from them, or they call it a donation of $135,000, so she lives very well as the former CEO. They also gave Benny Hinn $10,000.

Chapter 17

Daystar Television Network Marcus and Joni Lamb, Now Joni Weiss

"But whoso committeth adultery with a woman lacketh understanding: he that doeth it destroyeth his own soul."

Proverbs 6:32

The Daystar Network is located in Bedford, Texas, and as they say, everything is bigger in Texas. It was once located in Alabama, but "God" called, and Joni and Marcus answered the call and moved to the big "D" after selling the station to TBN in 1990.

They just finished a telethon (con-a-thon), and it was reported that twenty-five million dollars was pledged or squeezed from gullible miracle purchasers, who were promised healing, family salvation, favor, and financial breakthroughs. All from a God they say sees their generosity (selfishness) and is then obligated to respond to the filthy lucre laid at the feet of Marcus and Joni Lamb.

Ah, "Christian" TV is very lucrative, and it allows the owners to live the extravagant lifestyles of the rich and famous. Corporate jets, mansions, luxury cars, expensive clothes, plastic surgeries, drugs, hair transplants, and girlfriends.

Girlfriends? Yes, Marcus Lamb with all his crying and gymnastics was carrying on an affair with someone who worked at the network. Marcus must have loved going to the office. Talk about fringe benefits!

Marcus and Joni went on a PR campaign, even appearing on *Dr. Phil* to insinuate they may be being blackmailed. Here is a document from the police department as they investigated and found no blackmail or extortion.

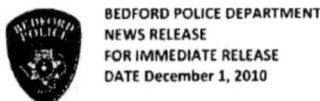

BEDFORD POLICE DEPARTMENT
NEWS RELEASE
FOR IMMEDIATE RELEASE
DATE December 1, 2010

CONTACT: Lt. Kirk Roberts
E_MAIL : kroberts@ci.bedford.tx.us
PHONE: (817) 952-2414

BEDFORD, TEXAS – We have been in contact with a representative of Day Star and the matter is currently under investigation.

We will have no comment on a pending investigation.

UPDATED
December 8, 2010

Bedford, Texas – After review of the details provided by Day Star, and consulting with the Tarrant County District Attorney's Office, there does not appear to be any criminal conduct under the Texas Law. As such, the Bedford Police Department has ended its investigation into the matter

After Marcus got caught, submission to Joni must have been a must. He chose to stay at the network and in the marriage, although it must have been some strange bedfellows there at the Lamb home. The ex-mistress was involved in a lawsuit, which was later dismissed. Here are some excerpts from the

court filings. You can find the court documents online filed by another plaintiff against Word of God Fellowship or Daystar. They are registered as a church.
https://www.scribd.com/document/49074307/daystar-lawsuit-021611

"In 2007, an employee of Daystar who reported to Plaintiff advised Plaintiff and another employee who was in charge of information systems, that he found emails clearly proving that Defendant Marcus D. Lamb and (blank) were having an illicit sexual relationship and that it had been going on for about seven years. In addition to many lewd statements, Defendant Marcus D. Lamb wrote in one of his emails that he could not wait to make her the next Marcus D. Lamb." (Quote from lawsuit).

One day on the air, Joni almost socked him as she grabbed the microphone he was holding. All because he was going to say something she did not want him to share. Whoa, I bet some frying pans fly at their house.

They were the masters of deception as they blamed the ex-employees to garner sympathy for Marcus. They outright lied about being blackmailed. The plaintiffs were asking for a financial settlement from their lawsuit, which is perfectly legal, and Joni and Marcus knew it. But the judgment of God would soon catch up at Daystar.

Marcus and his constant flattery of Joni was so fake!! Joni was gaining more and more weight; maybe she was frustrated in her role as Mrs. Lamb, but then $50,000,000 or more a year is a great incentive to stay married, even if she had to put up with Marcus. Joni later looked like a new woman when she married Doug Weiss; she lost a massive amount of weight and looked ten years younger. Confessing in a leaked audio to make-out sessions with Dr. Doug before they were married, she stated it was to see if there was a "connection."

Again, Joni freely participates in all the scamming, selling Jesus at any price. The Catholic church could be their model. Remember what indulgence selling did for them. It made them extremely wealthy. Money and fame are the heroin of ministry, and Marcus and Joni were addicted; they even trained their children in the art of the con as they also participate in the telethons. They must also like the lifestyle that they enjoy and cannot, or so it seems by watching them, break free from the influence of Mommy and Daddy. The lure of inheriting that network must be very strong.

The network now has at least 100 TV stations with satellite and cable coverage that potentially reaches over 100 million U.S. households in more than 200 countries. The estimated value of the network is a billion dollars, and that was according to Marcus Lamb and Jonathan. Here are some famous Marcus Lamb quotes:

"I believe there are 300 people just like Gideon's army of 300. These people are those that will give $77.

"And God is saying, 'Move today.' It could be that you need a new house! It could be that you need a better car! It could be that you need a promotion on the job... it could be that you've been praying for that son to get saved...You've been praying that God would restore your marriage...I say to you today, 'Don't just throw your seed. Sow your seed!' There is a difference. You can call up today and make a pledge and that's great! And I say, 'God bless you.' But if you don't have an intended purpose for that seed then all you did is throw that seed instead of sow that seed." (Daystar Spring Share-A-Thon, Dated: March 2005)

In a recent "Heart for the World" telethon, they were promising all kinds of miracles for your seeds (money). Marcus, with his phony, crying was saying all the wonderful things that he was hearing from God about how 700 people were to give a certain amount, and then seventy people were to give a certain amount. It was all wrapped up around God's holiest day, or so they say, the Jewish Day of Atonement.

What? Just what "holy days" does God have? Does He have special days when you must approach Him with financial offerings? He is hearing voices all right, but that is not Almighty God talking. It sounds more like the devil.

This particular scam has been very popular lately. The Jewish feast day scams. Most of the prosperity pimps have jumped on the very lucrative Jewish feast day bandwagon, presenting their God with offerings on holy days, or their God gets mad at you and won't bless you. Pitiful!

Marcus was scurrying around, sobbing, going to the phone banks, promising to hold your prayer requests in his hands, as if his prayers were better than yours because you sent God (Marcus) some money!!

The unsaved world must tune into these programs sometimes just to get some comic relief.

You might say, "Susan, why do you use the word pimps?" The Bible says they have gone a-whoring, that's why.

Judges 2:17
"And yet they would not hearken unto their judges, but they went a whoring after other gods, and bowed themselves unto them: they turned quickly out of the way which their fathers walked in, obeying the commandments of the LORD; but they did not so."

Deuteronomy 31:16
"And the LORD said unto Moses, Behold, thou shalt sleep with thy fathers, and this people will rise, and go a whoring after the gods of the strangers of the land whither they go to be among them, and will forsake me, and break my covenant which I have made with them."

Hosea 9:1
"Rejoice not, O Israel, for joy, as other people: for thou hast gone a whoring from thy God, thou hast loved a reward upon every corn floor."
Psalm 106:39

"Thus were they defiled with their own works, and went a whoring with their own inventions."

Ezekiel 6:9
"And they that escape of you shall remember me among the nations whither they shall be carried captives, because I am broken with their whorish heart, which hath departed from me, and with their eyes, which go a whoring after their idols: and they shall loathe themselves for the evils which they have committed in all their abominations."

Marcus Lamb passed away in November 2021 at the age of sixty-four from complications of Covid. It was a sad time for the family, as it was so unexpected.

Joni did not waste any time finding a new husband. She married the recently divorced Dr. Doug Weiss, who is known as a sex therapist, in June 2023. Doug was married to Lisa Weiss for over thirty years according to published reports. He filed for divorce about two months after Marcus died.

Joni started to plan to build a new 9,700 sq. ft. mansion worth about four million in March 2022 just down the road from her current mansion. She paid over a million dollars for the lot. Hard to believe that she was building it for herself, although she claims her relationship with Doug began much later in 2022.

After Joni and Doug married, they purchased a luxury beachfront Condo in Florida worth over three million dollars. They jet to Florida in the Daystar "ministry" jet, and Joni used the jet as the "Love Boat" while she dated

Doug. She took over twenty round trips to Colorado, where Doug lived at the time, and he still owns a house there valued at over one million dollars. Joni also owns a lake house in Texas valued at about $900,000.

Another financial scandal came to light when it was revealed that Daystar lost about twenty-five million in a crypto scheme perpetuated by con artist Sam Bankman-Fried, now in prison for his frauds. Daystar has filed suit, trying to recover their investment.

Financial documents from 2011 revealed that Daystar had about forty million in airtime sales, so it appears the telethons just make them richer and richer, bigger and bigger.

But they never have enough money, as now "Dr. Doug" and Joni pick up the miracle-selling mantle Marcus left behind

Daystar Jet

Lawsuit for Crypto Scheme

LOCAL NEWS

Church sues Silvergate Bank for losing $25 million deposit in FTX crypto-scheme

Building Lot Purchase for the New Mansion (note the date, three months after Marcus died), March 2022. Cost over $1 million

Daystar Television Network Marcus and Joni Lamb, Now Joni Weiss

Production Revenue	54,555
Commission	6,453
Other Rent Income	27,355
Service Charge Fee	493,981
Misc. Broadcasting Revenue	94,700
Total Other Broadcasting Revenue	677,043
Total Broadcasting Revenue	54,046,909

Merchandise/Other Revenue

Broadcasting revenue from 2011

	New Single Family
Status:	Issued
Project Name:	
IVR Number:	
Applied Date:	02/10/2023
Issue Date:	05/30/2023
District:	EAST
Assigned To:	
Expire Date:	03/11/2024
Square Feet:	9,738.00
Valuation:	$3,900,000.00

Building Permit for New $4 Million Mansion

Joni Lamb's Current Mansion, Texas

In November 2024, Jonathan and Suzy Lamb went public with allegations of a sexual abuse coverup at Daystar that involved their then-five-year-old daughter and a family member. Their claims created a firestorm for Joni Lamb and her network. Jonathan and Suzy allege that Marcus and Joni never fully investigated the sexual abuse claim.

Voice recordings and other important documentation was brought forward that exposed the corruption and financial abuses, especially by Joni Lamb.

It was reported by Jonathan Lamb that Joni spent over $100,00 on her honeymoon to Doug Weiss and that the ministry paid for it. Joni denied the allegation, yet who spends $100,000 on a honeymoon? She did not deny that.

Joni fired Suzy Lamb in 2023 for not reading a comment by a viewer praising Joni's new husband, Doug Weiss. Suzy and Jonathan objected to the new marriage and viewed it as adultery, and they did not want to compromise their religious beliefs, but Joni wanted to stage her new life with Doug to gain public approval no matter what the cost to her family.

Joni, in a meeting with Jimmy Evans, a well-known minister and a marriage counselor whose specialty is restoring marriages (but not Doug's), badgered Jonathan for about two hours, repeating the word "submit" over ninety times.

When Suzy who would not "submit" to the "voice of God" at Daystar, Joni, she was told to pack up and leave. Next Jonathan Lamb, the then-vice-president, was also told the same thing. He would have to praise Doug Weiss or face Joni's wrath.

Jimmy Evans acted like a bully, with archaic submission doctrines and stated that Joni Lamb was indeed the voice of God at Daystar. Jonathan Lamb wisely recorded the conversation, and had he not done so, it would have been hard to believe that such abuse actually goes on in these ministry kingdoms.

The scandal raises all sorts of questions about abuse and coverups in these mega-rich organizations. Programmers have been leaving the network, yet Joni continues her reckless behavior, unrepentant and as arrogant as ever.

The Miracle Sellers

Doug Weiss divorce document filed January 27, 2022, just two months after Marcus Lamb died, finalized May 31, 2022:

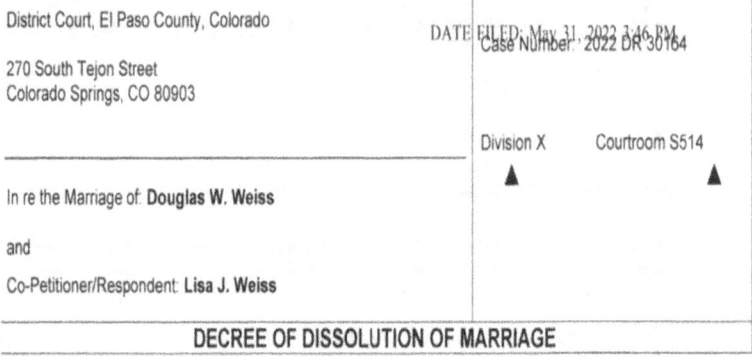

Deed for new building lot March 2022

Chapter 18
TBN-Trinity Broadcasting Network

"And the soul that turneth after such as have familiar spirits and after wizards, to go a whoring after them, I will even set my face against that soul and will cut him off from among his people."

Leviticus 20:6

TBN was co-founded by Paul and Jan Crouch in 1973, along with Jim and Tammy Bakker. Jim Bakker was the brains behind the founding of most of the major "Christian" networks. According to Jim Bakker's website, http://www.jimbakkershow.com, Jim became the founder and host of the first Christian talk show, *The 700 Club*, which is now the ministry of Pat Robertson. He also states that he was the first president and founder of TBN.

He is a clever businessman, even rebuilding his own life after spending about five years in a federal penitentiary and losing everything he owned, including his wife Tammy, who later divorced him, and she then married Roe Messner, the contractor who helped build PTL.

Tammy died of cancer in 2007. She left behind her daughter, Tammy Sue, who was working with her dad and his new wife, Lori at his ministry headquarters near Branson, Missouri, and their son, Jamie Charles, or Jay as he now calls himself, who is a Universalist, and who does not believe in hell. The children suffered, no doubt, from the sins of their parents.

Some of us can remember how we felt back then in 1987 when Jim Bakker, our brother in the Lord, was led away in handcuffs, crying; it was all too much. We, as the body of Christ, no longer felt safe; the men we had trusted let us down.

No, I do not approve of what Jim Bakker did, but on the human level, it was painful to watch and painful for him and his family. The media was extremely cruel, especially to his children. They were young, and they did nothing to deserve the hell they went through. And then there was Jerry Falwell, who the Bakers trusted, and he betrayed them with a hostile takeover of the ministry and the assets.

Most of what he built in Ft Mill, North Carolina, now stands in ruins. Once beautiful, it is a monument to the judgment of God on a ministry. Visitors to the abandoned buildings and grounds of Heritage USA share videos on YouTube of the Bakker's old amusement park.

I was there a few years after the fall, when Morris Cerullo was trying to buy the place. He was holding a telethon, and the TV studio was in shambles: stained curtains, leaky roofs, and overgrown landscaping. Just a mess! I remembered it from watching the *Jim and Tammy Show* or PTL as it was called back then. Jim had kept the place so beautiful. He had great skill as a businessman, but now it looked haunted.

Once a bustling theme park sitting on 2300 acres and with over six million visitors a year, it became the third most visited theme park in the United States.

As I drove around town, I noticed even the malls and the businesses surrounding Heritage were boarded up. The loss of PTL hurt many many people and their once-thriving businesses.

False prophet Rick Joyner now owns the hotel, and he runs his "ministry" there.

Jim Bakker stayed with the Crouchs for about a year during the founding of TBN, and then he moved on leaving the Crouchs to build their network, now the largest so-called "Christian" broadcaster in the world. Worth over a billion dollars and they still want more.

Now that Paul Senior and Jan are gone, Matt and his family have picked up the torch.

Eventually, God will judge this mess, and it will fall apart unless they repent and stop the money changing. Why is it so hard for a rich man to enter the Kingdom of Heaven? Yet Jesus Himself said it would be.

TBN could be a beacon for the real gospel of love that Jesus Christ wants us to have for others. I do not treat members of my own family the way TBN treats the members of God's family.

I do not tell my mother that if she gives me money, God will heal her, bring salvation to lost family members, or give her a breakthrough. What has happened to the church? The real church has become a remnant; you do not see the remnant on TV. TBN would not let me speak there, or any other real reformer, but God, in His infinite wisdom, allowed me to write this book.

We have a presence on the internet where we have reached a few million people with our radio broadcasts, websites, and video channels. Never once asking anyone for a donation, seed faith offering, or tithe.

God can speak to people directly about helping. I am not opposed to people in ministry receiving an offering or having partners or selling a book, but always do it with integrity.

TBN failed the test when the money started pouring in. Instead of using it wisely, they bought station after station, building after building, enriching themselves and losing out with God.

Paul Crouch Sr. was accused of having a homosexual affair with Enoch Lonnie Ford. Ford alleged he had an affair with the "Christian" broadcaster while employed by Crouch, even writing a book about it.

Mysteriously, Enoch Lonnie Ford and his manuscript have disappeared. Instead of defending himself, Paul Sr. paid hush money to Lonnie in the form of a settlement, not once but twice. Now that Paul is dead, maybe Lonnie will reappear, along with his manuscript.

In another recent interview, Paul Crouch Jr. confirmed that he had a conversation with his father about his same-sex attraction. Paul Sr. stated he was molested as a teenager by a male relative, and Jr. believed this led to his alcoholism and his struggle with homosexuality. According to Paul Jr., Jan Crouch knew Paul Crouch Sr. was gay.

Another person who knew was Brittany Crouch. In an unpublished autobiography given to Jackie Alnor, Brittany Crouch states, "In drastic contrast, listening to my grandmother's stories of her marriage was like listening to something out of an episode of 'Tales from the Crypt' – too horrifying and bizarre to be reality. Right before I was preparing to marry my college sweetheart, Michael, my grandmother kept telling me how lucky I was to have found someone so gentle and handsome. I commented that she hadn't done so bad herself with papa, which immediately sent a rage through her soul that I could see flare out of her eyes. She waved her hands in the air and said, 'Papa? Please!

He used to treat me like a punching bag! You wouldn't believe the sh-- he's put me through!' Clearly, I was a bit dumbfounded because, although I didn't really have a close relationship with my grandfather at this point, I couldn't imagine him ever being violent with anyone. I could see that he had a bit of a temper and a sharp tongue, but violent? I thought that would have been the worst of it but then she went on: 'Did you know I used to have to go lay myself behind his car to keep him from going out and having sex with other men?! He used to get so trashed he'd take our car to the public restrooms to solicit sex from men! I had to pick him up from there one time! It was disgusting!' Okay, she had me now – where exactly was she going with this?"

What a tragic legacy to leave behind. The televangelists should remember the famous biblical warning:

"Be not deceived; God is not mocked: for whatsoever a man soweth that shall he also reap."
Galatians 6:7

Did God ruin their reputation and good name by exposing them for misusing His gospel? Did He give them space to repent?

"A good name is better than precious ointment; and the day of death than the day of one's birth."
Ecclesiastes 7:1

He will send a whale just like he did to Jonah, who will swallow you up and hold you captive and then spit you out until you finally surrender. That Bible and its truths that you hold and preach out of cost Jesus His life, and it was no small price. That salvation that you experienced, that amazing grace, cannot be used to disgrace our Lord.

Some of the pimp preachers have sued internet ministries and have tried to have them shut down for exposing the corruption, especially in television ministry. Don't fear us, but fear God. Just like when the prophet Nathan pointed his finger at David and said, "Thou art the man-take heed," Your life is hanging in the balance. This scripture also comes to mind "for a bird of the air shall carry the voice, and that which hath wings shall tell the matter" (Ecclesiastes 10:20). The bird of the air today could now be the internet.

According to Wikipedia: "TBN owns 35 full-power television stations serving larger metropolitan areas in the United States; at its peak, the network also owned 252 [low-power television stations](), which are mixed among stations serving medium-sized cities and rural translator stations in order to maximize the network's reach as much as is permissible.

"TBN also has several hundred affiliate stations throughout the United States, although just 61 of these are full-power UHF or VHF stations; the rest are low-powered stations.
"Worldwide, TBN's channels are broadcast on 70 satellites and over 18,000 television and cable affiliates. The TBN networks are also streamed live on the internet globally."

How many TV studios do you need to preach the gospel? TBN owned many studios around the country, which were rarely used, some were in New York City, Nashville, Atlanta, Alabama, Miami, Dallas, Tustin, Santa Ana, Denver, and Tulsa. Some of these properties have been sold, and they now have many international studios as well.

The prosperity preachers will tell you that if you sow seeds to them, you will get even more money and then they can reach even more people, but as you can see, TBN got more money, and they greedily helped themselves.

Nashville Studio

Holyland Experience Before They Tore It Down

TBN – Trinity Broadcasting Network

Say something against TBN and they may slap a lawsuit on you, even suing their own granddaughter, and they have the money and the attorneys to do it. They will use both to harass you, spending over five million dollars in one year according to public documents. And yes, your donations go to pay attorneys for frivolous lawsuits. What is Christian about that?

They even televise Catholic masses and display false teacher after false teacher, scripture twisters, financial pimps, ridden with scandals, alleged adulterers and confessed adulterers, alleged homosexuals and confessed homosexuals. What a testimony.

Lately, Matt has been teaming up with Dr. Phil McGraw, who, along with his wife Robin, platformed mediums and psychics on his program, *The Dr. Phil Show*, even receiving a reading on his show from medium John Edwards. He received a psychic reading from psychic Char Margolis on another program.

Robin had a podcast that was named "I've Got a Secret," where she did a tarot card reading and conjured up spirits, yet they claim to be Christians. One episode with Robin that you can hear on YouTube was "The Secret to Your Tarot Fortune" with Angie Banicki. Another was "Celebrity Tarot Reader and Astrologist Predict Spring 2022" with astrologer Aliza Kelly and "Tarot Card Reading" with Angie Banicki and a numerologist. Robin was all in on these programs and was all in with her guests saying that it was "fun."

Phil teamed up with Matt Crouch to feature his Merit Street Media productions. Here is a quote from *PR Newswire*, April 2, 2024, about the partnership with TBN: "America's most-watched faith-and-family network, when they announced that a dynamic new partner channel, Merit Street Media, launched today, April 2, on cable, satellite,

TBN – Trinity Broadcasting Network

broadcast, and streaming platforms nationwide."

Dr. Phil emphasized that the teachings of the gospel have never been more important than they are right now, but many people need to witness those teachings in a practical modern-world setting. "I think you have to use language and examples that people can understand and relate to," he explained. "And that is the goal of Merit Street. We won't preach the Gospel, but we'll do our best each day to model it in an authentic way." He added: "I hope everyone who watches TBN understands that what we are providing through Merit Street is a fortification of the ministry of TBN. We're fellow-travelers on a very important mission."

Matt has no discernment! Why platform people who have promoted witchcraft and then try to pass them off as believers to the family of God?

God says in His word He would even make your enemies to be at peace with you if you do right in His eyes. We can't say that about TBN, so the next time you are tempted to send them a donation, find someone who really needs some help. TBN does not need another donation.

Please, TBN, repent or go away- please!!

Some Paul Crouch quotes:
"I'm tired of sad heresy hypocrites blocking the bridges when the harvest is perishing out there and God's calling the party to get together. Let Him {God} sort out all this doctrinal doo-doo, I don't care about it." (Praise the Lord: Dated: 1 December 2005)

"God spoke to me clearly and said, 'Did I give my son Jesus on the cross expecting nothing in return?' God bankrupted heaven and gave the best gift he could give. He gave the best offering he could give. What did God need? He needed sons and daughters, he gave the very thing he needed. You can bring God a gift fully expecting something."

(TBN, Praise-A-Thon, dated: 31 March 2004)

"God, we proclaim death to anything or anyone that will lift a hand against this network and ministry that belongs to you, God. It is your work, your idea, it is your property, it is your airwaves, it is your world. We proclaim death to anything that would stand in the way of God's great voice of proclamation to the whole world. In the name of Jesus and all the people said Amen!"

(TBN, dated: 7 November 1997)

"If you have been healed or saved or blessed through TBN and have not contributed to the station, you are robbing God and will lose your reward in heaven."

(Dated: 4 August 1997)
https://www.azquotes.com/author/41873-Paul_Crouch

"I think God's given up on a lot of that old rotten Sanhedrin religious crowd, twice dead,

plucked up by the roots. I think they're damned and on their way to hell and I don't think there's any redemption for them...the heresy hunters that want to find a little more of illegal doctrine in some Christian's eye and pluck that little mote out of their eye when they've got the whole forest in their own lives and in their own eyes. I say to hell with you! Oh hallelujah."
https://www.biblebb.com/files/wrdfaith.htm

"Get out of God's way, quit blocking God's bridges or God's gonna shoot you if I don't! I refuse to argue any longer with any of you out there. Don't even call me. If you want to argue doctrine, if you want to straighten out somebody over here, if you want to criticize Ken Copeland for his preaching on faith, or Dad Hagin. Get out of my life! I don't even want to talk to you or hear you. I don't want to see your ugly face! Get out of my face in Jesus' name."

(Paul Crouch, dated: 2 April 1991)

"I'm eradicating the word Protestant even out of my vocabulary... I'm protesting nothing... it's time for Catholics and non-Catholics to come together as one in the Spirit and one in the Lord."

(*Praise the Lord* program, TBN, dated: 17 October 1989)

"Do you know what else that's settled then tonight? This hue and cry and controversy that has been spawned by the devil to try to bring dissension within the body of Christ that we are gods. I am a little god....I am a little god. Critics be gone."

(*Praise the Lord* program, TBN, dated: 5 February 1986)

In 2017, TBN and its affiliates took in a windfall of $634 million so far from the sale of its television broadcast spectrum. The non-profit certainly turned a big profit!

Chapter 19

The Word Network or the Un-Word Network

"Thy word is a lamp unto my feet, and a light unto my path."

Psalm 119:105

Now if you ever want to see some very strange "Christians," turn on the Word Network. One of the big players of the past was George Bloomer, who would wipe his anointed sweat on your money. Now that's a whopper. He wrote a book on witchcraft and how to protect yourself from demons, but apparently, George did not read it himself! Who will protect us from George?

Paul Crouch Jr. was a network executive there and served as VP in charge of program development after being fired or resigned from his parents' network, TBN; he was given the boot along with his whole family. Now Matt Crouch and his brood will pick up the spoils, and it is quite the lucrative haul if there ever was one.

Hell would have to freeze over before Paul Jr. would ever step foot on the unholy grounds of TBN. I am sure Matt is not into sharing.

You may think your family fights over money, but that is nothing compared to the billion dollars that is at stake over at TBN. Jesus said that the love of money is the root of all evil, and amen to that.

Paul Jr. now remarried to Brenda, and he revamped the Word Network, and it was not for the good. It is a baby of the TBN model of gospel pimping and scamming. Delivering one false prophet after another.

They too have mastered the seed-faith-a-thon, or give God (the Word Network) some money, and God grants you debt cancellations, healings, family salvations, and on and on. I thought maybe Paul Crouch

Jr. could make a fresh start after being at TBN and knowing full well how the game is played, but no, he does not turn away from what he learned all those years from TBN. They continue at the Word Network, duping the simple, using the name of Jesus, and how sad it is!

Paul was fired from the Word Network as God was rocking his boat. He now is doing video production with his son.

My hope for Paul Crouch Jr. is that he could take his name and use his talents, and they are many, to reject the other Jesus that is taught by men and women who have no regard for God's people. This is a time for him to shrug off the old man and be his own person. I am sure it is not easy to be a junior.

The Un-Word Network is owned by Kevin Adell and is based in Southfield, Michigan, just outside of Detroit, and it was founded in 2000. It now also has a studio in Orange, California. Adell owns over 100 automobiles, many valuable collectibles. He is a wealthy man and currently has put the network up for sale.

One of the programmers featured on the Word Network is Tony Alamo, a convicted pedophile who took child brides and was in prison serving a 175-year sentence when he died in 2017 at age eighty-two. They currently play his sermons. Obviously, they do not vet their content providers.

Chapter 20

TCT Network and Golden Eagle Broadcasting

"Thy prophets have seen vain and foolish things for thee: and they have not discovered thine iniquity, to turn away thy captivity; but have seen for thee false burdens and causes of banishment."

Lamentations 2:14

Garth and Tina Coonce launched TCT in 1977. Their religious TV network broadcasts the prosperity gospel throughout the Midwest. Garth passed away in January, 2023 and the stations mainly feature their children and grandchildren.

If you have ever watched this network, you will see that they too have learned the art of the Christian scam. Or how to get money from your pocket into theirs, so that they could own even more stations. After all, we need to see the same people on all the networks, day after day, and the same scams day after day; yes, we must have more "Christian" television.

TCT owns many other television stations. The family, Garth, his wife Tina, their daughter Julie, and her husband were paid over $800,000 in salaries in 2022. One year, their travel expenses alone were over $900,000. So, seed faith has been good to them. In 2022, they took in over eleven million in income according to their 990 filing.

GEB America (formerly known as Golden Eagle Broadcasting) is a digital satellite television network, which airs primarily Christian and family safe programming. Oral Roberts founded it in 1996. GEB America is owned by Oral Roberts University and is headquartered in Tulsa, Oklahoma. (source: Wikipedia).

You can see that Golden Eagle, or GEB, is a clone of all the rest of the compromised church TV stations. Once owned by Oral Roberts, it was another great loss for Richard, who, like the prodigal son, squandered away his riches.

They actually have services from the Mabee Center at ORU where they teach the students seed faith and how to buy and sell miracles. Not a good way to raise up the next generation of believers and ministers. Could they at least set a godly example for the students there?

How low is too low? They bring in preachers who do not know the Word to teach young students the ways of the world. Sell Jesus at any cost. Could you at least get some real men and women of integrity in there to set a standard for the next generation? (In 2023,

ORU took in $184,000,000 according to their 990 filing.)

Chapter 21
Toufik Benedictus "Benny" Hinn

"How long shall this be in the heart of the prophets that prophesy lies? yea, they are prophets of the deceit of their own heart;"

Jeremiah 23:26

Here comes the medicine man and his bag of tricks. Now, what man would want to imitate a dead woman?

Yet Toufik, Benny, uses the voice inflections of the late Kathryn Kuhlman, even visiting her grave to get some of her anointing. Benny claims he never even met Kathryn, yet he speaks glowingly of her as if they were once the best of friends.

Toufik was born in Jaffa, of Armenian and Greek descent. He claimed his father was the mayor of Jaffa, but that claim was critically challenged by the authors of the book, *The Confusing World of Benny Hinn*, G. Richard Fisher and M. Kurt Goedelman.

Another book that documents the false persona of Toufik is *Fake Faith Healers* by Yves Brault, who had close encounters of a very strange kind with Hinn.

Toufik moved to Canada with his family as a teenager and supposedly was born again, and he began his miracle crusades or healing ministry as a young man a few years later.

He moved to Orlando, Florida, and founded "Orlando Christian Center," which he later sold to Clint Brown, or Clint took on the debt, as was reported in the *Orlando Sentinel*. Clint, a spiritual son of Rod Parsley, also served as an amour bearer or brow wiper of the sinister Mike Murdock.

Clint later divorced his wife, his house went into foreclosure, and the bankrupt church that he bought from Hinn was sold at a foreclosure auction.

Toufik, Benny, was smart enough to get Clint to take over the almost six-million-dollar debt, and he got out of Dodge to head for California to build his healing gardens amusement park, which never got off the ground.

He built a multimillion-dollar mansion there, purchased a jet, fancy luxury automobiles, and a million-dollar divorce from his wife Suzanne, who he later remarried at the Holy Land Experience in Orlando, Florida, once owned by TBN, which has recently been torn down and sold.

Hinn was desperate during this time because his "ministry" was suffering great financial losses due to his d-i-v-o-r-c-e and the photo that appeared in the *National Enquirer* of the not-yet-divorced Hinn and Paula White, holding hands while in Rome on supposed Vatican business.

And no, the photo was not photoshopped; it was real, even though it came from the *Enquirer*.

Benny's nephew was quoted as saying in a recent statement posted on Twitter that Paula and Benny were at a Hinn family Christmas party before the Rome trip, so apparently, it was more than a friendship. Here is his tweet:

> Costi Hinn, October 14, 2019:
> "But I've shared a family Christmas with her before the divorce was final, then watched them spin the PR lie
> to millions, twist biblical parameters, and slowly creep back into the mainstream."

Hinn later begged for money, saying his divorce attorneys were billing him over $800,000. Who spends that kind of money on a divorce? He and Suzanne were supposed to be in "the ministry," so why couldn't they just talk things out?

No, they had to spend over $800,000 on lawyers. Needless to say, the divorce was costly. Benny said that he lost his California mansion and many, many partners. So, he remarried Suzanne and swore to the public she would be at his side in the ministry, but you rarely ever see her with Benny. Poor Suzanne had to drug herself in the first marriage, even going to the Betty Ford Clinic to kick her pill habit. Benny could not even help his own wife, but honestly, how does she tolerate all of his phoniness? Living a lie with the fake Toufik, Benny?

Maybe the pills were an escape from reality, a side effect of the fake ministry built on Benny's constant lying about the Lord Jesus to fund their very lavish lifestyle. Mansions, jewels, presidential suites, expensive private jets, maids, cooks, tailormade clothing, yet none of that made Suzanne happy, and she became a drug addict. Their daughter Jessica also suffered a nervous breakdown, which she herself has testified to.

It must be very difficult, and if you have any conscience at all to live a lie and then to have your children follow in the footsteps of a liar and a cheat, very difficult. Why would any mother subject her children to this chicanery or this use of trickery?

My criterion for recognizing wolves is if they cannot be honest with their fundraising, then we must reject them if we are ever to see a complete reformation.

Hinn also has Catholic leanings, if he is not one himself. After the death of Pope John Paul, Benny was seen standing in front of Saint Peter's in Rome, selling a video produced by his ministry about the dead pope's life.

Hinn also likes to wear a Roman collar. He is so religious. This is the power of suggestion, as it makes him appear to be some kind of reverend, but only God is Reverend. Obviously, we know Toufik is just a man with no healing power of his own, as only Jesus

Christ himself is a miracle worker. Yet, Benny loves the praises of man; he also loves money.

Toufik, Benny, loves to sell miracles to foolish people who would actually believe that he is some sort of a holy man, yet he has learned the old Catholic practice of indulgence selling.

Toufik was followed by the local news channel in Orlando to a foreign location as Tony Pipitone from WKMG, channel 6, reported on the story during the nightly news.

Toufik was seen on video passing a hookah pipe to Steve Brock, his singer, and his personal assistant, David Delgado, who later died of a heroin overdose.

And again, the photo was not doctored; the report appeared on channel 6 TV news, and they were not sued by Hinn.

"There's been a darker side to Hinn and his organization. In 1998 two members of his inner circle died of heroin overdoses. In 1999, after one of his many vows of reform, he fired several board members and hired an ex-cop named Mario C. Licciardello to do an internal investigation of his ministry.

"Licciardello was the brother-in-law of Carman, the popular Christian singer, so many think Hinn considered him 'safe.' But Licciardello did such a good job - taking hundreds of depositions and getting to the bottom of the heroin use - that Hinn then sued him.

"While Licciardello was still his head of security, the ministry filed a lawsuit demanding that all his files be turned over and sealed, because their public release could result in the end of the ministry.

"One day before Hinn was supposed to give his deposition in this case, Licciardello had a mysterious heart attack and died. The Hinn

organization made an out-of-court settlement with Licciardello's widow, which included sealing the court papers."
https://www.dmagazine.com/publications/d-magazine/2003/august/the-heretic/

Toufik Hinn, just who is this man? Does any real Christian use the tactics that Hinn employs to solicit donations? The answer is no.

He promotes the likes of Todd Coontz, Mike Murdock, Morris Cerullo, Steve Munsey, and his latest find, false prophet and New Age psychic, Brian Carn. Toufik is as phony as his name, Benny.

In March 2015, the then-sixty-two-year-old Benny was hospitalized for heart failure. After spending about a week in the hospital and time in intensive care, he was released.

Although Benny denies having a heart attack, his heart was attacked. You would think that after coming very close to meeting his Maker,

Benny would have turned over a new leaf. But no, he is up to his old tricks, deceiving the sheep for his own gain and still with a smile on his face.

But Benny will not be smiling when Jesus says to him, "Depart from me. I never knew you!!"

In July 2024, Suzanne Hinn filed for divorce for the second time. What will become of Benny as his woes increase?

Suzanne Hinn Divorce Filing

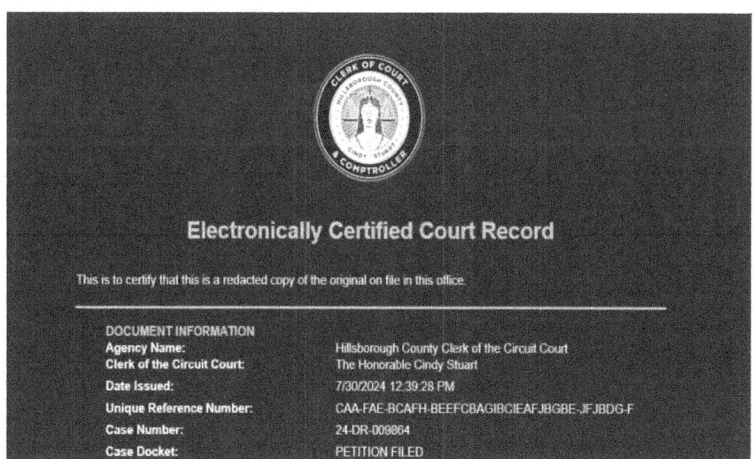

CASE NUMBER: 24-DR-009864
HINN, SUZANNE vs HINN, BENEDICTUS

Case Number: 24-DR-009864
Uniform Case Number: 292024DR009864A001HC
Filed On: 2024-07-26
Case Type: Dissolution of Marriage
Case Status: Open

Defendant: HINN, BENEDICTUS
Amount Due: $0.00

CASE PARTY INFORMATION

Party Type	Name	Attorney	Attorney Contact

CASE JUDGE INFORMATION

Judge Assigned	Division	Date	Reason
	Tampa	07/26/2024	

CASE EVENT INFORMATION

Event Date	Doc Index	Charge Number	Title
07/26/2024	8		Summons (Initial Case Filing) "Petitioner: HINN, SUZANNE"
07/26/2024	7		PETITION FILED "Petitioner: HINN, SUZANNE"
07/26/2024	6		NOTICE OF RELATED CASE "Petitioner: HINN, SUZANNE"
07/26/2024	5		DESIGNATION OF CURRENT MAILING AND E-MAIL ADDRESS "Petitioner: HINN, SUZANNE"
07/26/2024	4		NOTICE OF APPEARANCE "Petitioner: HINN, SUZANNE"
07/26/2024	3		DH513 FORM "Petitioner: HINN, SUZANNE"
07/26/2024	2		CIVIL COVER SHEET "Petitioner: HINN, SUZANNE"
07/26/2024	1		SRS NEW CASE FILED

Benny purchased a beach condo in Florida for over $2.5 million in 2023; he also owns millions of dollars in other real estate around the country.

Chapter 22
Morris and David Cerullo

Like father, like son, and David Cerullo is a clone of his con artist father, Morris. The family business has been very lucrative for the Cerullos. David's wife, Barbara, looks like a Stepford wife as she appears by his side, nodding yes to what she knows are lies and snake oil salesman tricks.

Teresa Cerullo also enjoyed the part as Morris pawed over her and called her momma. It appeared so phony!

Here is a short bio on Morris's early life from Wikipedia:

"Morris was born in Passaic, New Jersey in 1931, his parents were killed in an automobile accident when he was two.

"Because his father had Jewish heritage he was then raised in an orthodox Jewish orphanage in Clifton, New Jersey.

"He graduated from Divinity school in 1953 and was later ordained with the Assemblies of God."

I first became familiar with Morris when I saw him on "Christian" television in the early eighties. Morris was right out of the twilight zone with all his talk of visions and heavenly visitations; he was special.

I was on his mailing list for a while, and soon I was receiving the slickest-sounding appeal letters. Morris always needed more money. He was anointed, and after all, because of it, he was entitled.

I saw Morris in person sometime in the late eighties when he was trying to buy PTL, the old Heritage USA property previously owned by Jim and Tammy Bakker.

The vultures swooped down quickly to pick the remains of the now-devastated theme park after Jim Bakker was accused of adultery. He was accused of using ministry money to pay off Jessica Hahn, the woman he met in a Florida hotel for a brief but costly fling. The payoff was arranged with the help of Richard Dortch, and Jessica was supplied by John Wesley Fletcher.

Jessica became a celebrity, even appearing in *Playboy*. And you know what that all means. Jessica hinted that she slept with Hugh Hefner, and it appears that he did not help her out of the kindness of his heart. All the publicity made Jessica a millionaire. It was all a very seedy affair, but as the Bible says, your sin will find you out. She once worked for Pastor Gene Profeta. The father of the psychic hotline prophetess, Dayna Muldoon. I pulled into the haunted entrance of PTL, where an old billboard stood with the faded faces of Jim and Tammy Bakker, and I made my way to the area where the telethon was being held.

The building was in bad shape, as a hurricane had blown through there and damaged the roofs, which now leaked profusely.

The once-beautiful curtains were now stained, and you could smell the mold. I had volunteered to answer the phones as the pledges were called in. Morris's right-hand man was rude, and he insulted me when I wanted to leave. He told us to get ready as Morris made his $10,000 pitch, but when Morris made it, we could hear him, and he acted like the Holy Ghost just spoke to him about it, although we had been warned it would happen. I wanted to get out of there fast as I realized he was a phony.

The Cerullos purchased the old PTL television network from the bankruptcy court, a steal for seven million dollars, now known as INSP, The Inspiration Network, which is no inspiration at all.

He also purchased the property in Fort Mill, South Carolina, which included a hotel and numerous buildings in partnership with a Malaysian business group. The Malaysian businessmen later bought him out, and the property continued to face financial problems.

Heretic Rick Joyner bought the property and now runs a semi-insane asylum with bizarre manifestations, and they call it a church. It was reported to me by someone who attended Rick's church and was an eyewitness to many of the false prophecies and the endorsement of so-called prophet Paul Cain. Cain was an active homosexual and also had a problem with alcohol. Yet, he was accepted by many in charismatic ministry circles.

As I was driving through the town, I noticed many of the local businesses were now closed. Victims of the PTL tragedy. Hotels and malls which were built during the heyday were now boarded up.

Jim Bakker is now building a mini PTL in the area around Branson, Missouri.

Now back to Morris, the man of many scams who is now building a monument to his greatness in California, The Legacy Center. Morris even wants his scamming ministry to go on after his death. What?

Morris has a hypnotic voice. He has joined the list of one of the worst pimp preachers who has ever lived. You would think that in this year of our Lord, people would realize they are being sold miracles, which are really free for the asking.

But with no conscience, because it has been seared, Morris and David continue the charade as "ministers" of the Lord Jesus Christ. In 2005, Morris was indicted by a grand jury for failure to pay income taxes. His son, Mark Stephen Cerullo, was also charged with burglary in 1990, with a reported theft at a home improvement store. Mark died in 1993 at the age of thirty-six.

The recently purchased property in San Diego, California, was also to be used as a training center for ministers. No, please, no more training of pimp preachers! No more!!

Morris Cerullo passed away in 2020. Previously on his website, you could view a very creepy video presentation of his grandiose plans for his monument.

Here are some of Morris's outrageous claims:

Cerullo has claimed many things, including that, at the age of only fourteen, he was led out of an orphanage by two angelic beings who transported him to heaven for a personal meeting with God. According to this "vision," God informed Cerullo that, in the future, he would be capable of giving prophecy.

"Did you know that, from the beginning of time, the whole purpose of God was to reproduce Himself? Who are you? Come on, who are you? Come on, say it: 'Sons of God!' Come on, say it! And what does work inside us, brother, is that manifestation of the

expression of all that God is and all that God has. And when we stand up here, brother, you're not looking at Morris Cerullo; you're looking at God. You're looking at Jesus." (Morris Cerullo, *The End time Manifestation of the Sons of God*)
https://www.youtube.com/watch?v=w8SdEaMfRIc

"The world will experience the greatest economic turmoil in history, we are going to see in this decade a complete collapse of the present world monetary system. It will make the crash of 1929 seem like a picnic."

All this was to happen by 1994, but it never happened! Oddly enough, cult leader and the man who led over 900 people to drink cyanide-laced Kool-Aid said the same thing. Looking at Jim Jones was like looking at God.

Morris was building the Legacy Center in San Diego, California, and the brochure, showed that he had a very high opinion of himself. Through a very stunning multimedia presentation, visitors will witness the drama of God, imparting into Morris Cerullo's spirit that His heartbeat is wrapped up in one word: SOULS. The center of the Rotunda will feature an immense, life-sized mural that will lead visitors through the amazing life and ministry of Morris Cerullo.

The Israel Pavilion and March of Prophecy
The Israel Pavilion will feature life-size replicas of some of the historic sites of Israel and will also showcase the March of Prophecy. This visually depicts God's plan for the ages from the beginning of time to the return of Christ.

The Walk-Through the Bible will be dedicated to experiencing the power and might of God's holy Word, as the Bible comes alive in this fully encapsulated auditorium. "Breathtaking, computer-generated video images will fly past visitors from all directions--beginning with creation itself--as God speaks this world into existence. Before the voyage comes to an end, Jesus, in a true-to-life, holographic form, will make a personal invitation to receive Him as Lord and Savior.

"Located in sunny San Diego, California, and created to be an elegant complement to the graceful architecture of the Morris Cerullo International Center, the campus will be adorned with gorgeous plants and foliage, soothing waterfalls, elegant pools art structures, and engravings in homage to God's amazing beauty." This was all stated in the brochure promoting the Legacy Center.

Just what kind of "legacy" are you leaving behind, Morris? The audio and video evidence of your scripture twisting and your heretical teachings on seed faith, prosperity, first fruits offerings, Pentecost offerings, and your shameful appeal letters?

Legacy Center in San Diego, California

If you ever happen to view the Un-Inspiration Network, one of the people you will see is the master of the seed-faith scam, Mike Murdock, selling his wares. A full choir will be praising some Lord as they make their sales pitch for money. They even use students from Southeastern College as props in this madness.

Mike will sit there with Morris's clone, David Cerullo, as they discuss how God wants to bless you by sending them money!

Housing an elaborate production facility on ninety-three acres, David Cerullo planned to build big, but according to Wikipedia, one aspect of it has yet to pan out.

"As of mid-2009, about 200 of the company's 330 employees work at the site. Only two of nine promised projects have been completed or even started. Construction on condominiums, supposed to begin in July 2008, is now 'long into the future' due to the effects of decreased giving and economic decline."

Now the network can reach over 69% of all households in the USA, broadcasting secular and religious programming.

Here is some financial information about the network and seed faith pays big dividends.

Throughout most of the 1990s, the network did not ask for donations on the air, unlike many other religious TV stations. Instead, it generated revenue by selling advertising and airtime for programs produced by other ministries. In 1999, the network began soliciting donations from the public. That year, gifts were about $200,000. By 2008, they were about forty million.

In 2007, the network's revenues were more than sixty-nine million. Profits between 2002 and 2006 totaled thirty-nine million.

In 2013, Chief Executive David Cerullo, Morris Cerullo's son, was paid more than five million, making him the best-paid leader of any religious charity tracked by watchdog groups.

His wife Barbara was paid over $276,000, and their children, Ben and Becky, were also employed by the company; Ben was paid more than $200,000 that year.

Cerullo and Barbara built a 12,000-square-foot home, valued between two and four million dollars, near Salem, South Carolina. Critics say the construction is inappropriate, given the financial resources of the network.

Employees complained about cutbacks, even though the Cerullos did not cut back on whatever their souls lusted after.

Morris bought himself a Gulfstream jet estimated to be worth fifty million dollars. He travels in style. Reportedly, one of his mansions is worth over twelve million. A friend of mine from London, England, with a wife and three children donated his home to Cerullo, and he took it. They wound up living in a crowded studio apartment for a while, and Morris went to his 12,000-square-foot mansion.

Morris was sued by former employee, John Paul Warren. This is a quote from a newspaper story about the Cerullos and John

Paul Warren, who tried to sue Cerullo for defrauding his partners:

"Cerullo's antagonist is determined that Cerullo be exposed to the Christian community for his actions. He says he tried for nearly two years to get Cerullo to submit to Church leadership for correction, but predictably Cerullo refused.

"He says he traveled with Cerullo throughout the world and witnessed his actions firsthand. He asked Cerullo to return millions of dollars to the donors, but predictably Cerullo refused. So Warren felt he had no other choice but to take him to court.

"The Appellate Court of the State of California ruled Jan. 3, 2002, that Cerullo, whose Morris Cerullo World Evangelism (MCWE) is based in San Diego, had immunity from litigation under the First Amendment, which precludes the courts from getting involved in the internal disputes of religious groups. MCWE said that the allegations are '100 percent without merit' -- cited the ministerial exemption when it sought a preliminary judgment dismissing Warren's claims."

This article appeared on the PFO website as another former employee, Harry Turner, sued. He did receive a settlement, but it was an out-of-court settlement.

"In recent months, faith healer Morris Cerullo has found himself and his San Diego based ministry targeted with various lawsuits and allegations of wrongdoing.

"Last year, John Paul Warren, a former executive for the Morris Cerullo World Evangelism (MCWE) ministry, filed a suit in San Diego Superior Court. Warren charges Cerullo with 'fraud, violation of the California Labor Code and misuse of Warren's confidential 5,000 name mailing list,'" according to a lengthy news report in the May 2001 issue of *Charisma* Magazine.

While officials at Cerullo's ministry refuse to address the particulars of the lawsuit, they did state that Warren's accusations are "100 percent without merit." They also allege that prior to filing the suit, Warren demanded $2.2 million from the organization to avoid his litigation and that he has refused to enter into binding Christian arbitration with his grievances.

Warren's suit indicts Cerullo, saying that at a January 1997 meeting, the evangelist solicited $1,500 gifts from donors to MCWE. According to the news report, "In return [for the donation], Warren said MCWE promised to provide them with a satellite dish allowing access to its global prayer satellite network as well as other organizational events." Warren said that donors were never given the satellite dishes they were promised. Cerullo's attorney responded to the charge, saying "the ministry made it clear to donors that the satellite dish offer was contingent on negotiations with system providers," the magazine reported.

Warren, who worked for the Cerullo ministry from March 1998 until being fired in October 1999, also alleges that he was lured to the ministry with promises of becoming Cerullo's "partner" and eventual "successor."

The attraction of those promises, he says, convinced him to abandon his own ministry and hand over his own list of donors to MCWE. He further maintains that his name was removed from being considered as a possible candidate for pastor of an Assemblies of God congregation in Oregon after the church called Cerullo's ministry for a personal reference.

A previous lawsuit filed against Cerullo has been settled out of court. Another former MCWE employee, Harry Turner, reached an undisclosed settlement with the ministry. Turner, a former vice president who resigned in November 1999, also charged the evangelist with "lies and fraud ... to his donors." Turner, like Warren, also requested money to settle the complaints short of litigation. Turner had demanded $800,000 to prevent the lawsuit.

During depositions for the Turner lawsuit, "Robert Killion, Cerullo's chief financial officer, admitted that the federal government was investigating allegations of mail fraud at Cerullo's ministry," Charisma reported. Also revealed was that "Davis Frast, a public information officer and inspector with the Postal Inspection Service, said that his agency has received complaints about Cerullo's ministry and the agency is in the first stages of an investigation." (San Diego Union-Tribune/6/24/2000
By Alex Roth)

Officials at MCWE contend that both lawsuits are attempts to extort money and energy from the ministry. Now, who are the real extortioners here?

The Legacy Center now operates as a hotel and spa in San Diego, California. Meetings are also held there, but the big plans that Morris had have yet to come to pass.

Chapter 23

Robert Morris

"For thou hast trusted in thy wickedness: thou hast said, None seeth me. Thy wisdom and thy knowledge, it hath perverted thee; and thou hast said in thine heart, I am, and none else beside me."

Isaiah 47:10

Robert Morris was riding high as the pastor of Gateway Church in 2024. Wealthy beyond belief, as they had nine locations in Texas and one in Wyoming, collecting millions in tithes and offerings. Boasting they had over 100,000 attending the services.

Robert taught that one must give God ten percent of your income or be cursed. Guess he did not read the scripture in Galatians that we were redeemed from the curse when Jesus died.

"Christ hath redeemed us from the curse of the law, being made a curse for us: for it is written, Cursed is every one that hangeth on a tree:"
Galatians 3:13

He bragged about giving away everything he owned at one point, house, cars, bank accounts, etc., but he forgot one very important detail about his past.

Cindy Clemishire came forward in 2024 publicly and gave her testimony about how Robert Morris began molesting her at age twelve and the molestation continued for over four years while he was married with a small son.

He was also active in public ministry at the time. Cindy later confessed to her family what Robert had been doing to her all those years. She suffered emotionally from this wicked abuse for many years.

Robert's wife, Debbie, knew what he had done after he was confronted, and so did his pastor. He should have been arrested, and he should have never been accepted as a pastor or in any sort of public ministry platform. Yes, God forgives, but men who abuse children sexually should never hold positions of trust.

Morris resigned reluctantly from Gateway Church, never fully confessing about what he had done to Cindy. He confessed to a moral failure with a young lady, but she was twelve. He was not truthful in his most recent confession and cannot be trusted.

He was twenty years old when he started working for James Robison, another well-known televangelist. He began holding meetings for James in high schools. Sometime later, he began molesting Cindy while he was staying at her home with her parents.

He reportedly took two years off from public ministry so that he could be restored, but that has been disputed. He was later made an elder at the church he was attending, even though the pastor there knew about his molestation of Cindy. It was sick, and how Morris was ever elevated to being a pastor and a well-known televangelist is even sicker. We can thank God that this man will never hold a leadership position again in the body of Christ.

Morris Property Holdings

Robert Morris has a ranch in Jacksboro, Texas with over 240 acres of land. He sold his house in Westlake for over three million. He also sold his house in Colleyville for over three million. He also owns a lake house worth over one million.

Morris was arrested in March of 2025 and indicted on five counts of lewd and indecent acts on a child.

Chapter 24
Mike Bickle

"And the burden of the LORD shall ye mention no more: for every man's word shall be his burden; for ye have perverted the words of the living God, of the LORD of hosts our God."

Jeremiah 23:36

Mike Bickle rose to fame by starting the International House of Prayer in Kansas City. A church with a 24/7 prayer room and a specific focus on prophecy and prophets. Here is a quote from their website.

"On May 7, 1999, the International House of Prayer of Kansas City (IHOPKC) was founded by Mike Bickle and twenty full-time "intercessory missionaries," who cried out to God in prayer with worship for thirteen hours each day. Four months later, on September

19, 1999, prayer and worship extended to the full 24/7 schedule."

It became a haven for men like Paul Cain and Bob Jones. Cain was a practicing homosexual and an alcoholic, who Bickle gave credibility to throughout the years. Bob Jones was molesting women, using his prophetic "gift" to do unspeakable things to women, yet Bickle often referenced him and appeared to respect him, but Bickle himself had secrets.

In 2023, a woman came forward and claimed that Bickle began molesting her in the 1990s. Another woman, Tammy Woods, came forward with her testimony of how Bickle began molesting her at age fourteen. It went on for a few years, and Bickle was in public ministry and married at the time.

He stepped down from his position at IHOPKC after much public pressure. How did he ever rise to such prominence with all his false teachings and cult-like behavior?

He had a false humility concerning money, even though the organization took in tens of millions of dollars over the years. He bragged about driving an older Honda and living in a duplex, even though they, IHOPKC and their affiliates were rich, rich, rich. (See examples below) (Source: ECFA)

So, as the body of Christ, we cannot tolerate child molesters and people who have a history of sexual perversion to be our leaders. We must raise up and set a standard for what we expect from those that we place our trust in.

International House of Prayer--Forerunner Christian Fellowship

Kansas City, MO
Founded: 1999
Current Status: Member
Member Since: April 1, 2016
Click here to view the certified church's profile

Comparative Financial Data			
	06/30/15	06/30/16	06/30/17
Revenue			
Cash Donations	$15,947,620	$14,512,963	$14,624,670
Noncash Donations	$0	$16,054	$406,203
Other Revenue	$8,800,472	$8,756,707	$6,431,826
Total Revenue	$24,748,092	$23,285,724	$21,462,699

Money that was taken in from 2015-2017, over $70 million (ECFA)

In a report that was recently released it was found that there were at least 17 victims of Mike Bickle's abuse including rape. Astonishing and disturbing. We thank God that the victims came forward to expose this monster.

https://religionnews.com/2025/02/05/report-details-17-cases-of-abuse-by-mike-bickle-ihopkc-founder/

Chapter 25

Glossary of Other Miracle Sellers

or

Commentary on More Pimp Preachers Who Have Also Gone A-Whoring

"In thee have they taken gifts to shed blood; thou hast taken usury and increase, and thou hast greedily gained of thy neighbours by extortion, and hast forgotten me, saith the Lord GOD."

Ezekiel 22:12

"Horror hath taken hold upon me because of the wicked that forsake thy law."

Psalm 119:53

Jentezen Franklin: A talented saxophone player with a whole lot of charisma, but Jentezen has joined the ranks of the pimp preacher, loving fame and fortune more than Jesus. He was doing cheerleading for many so-called "Christian" TV networks, preaching about how to give God money or "precious seed," and then all of your dreams would come true. Born in 1962, Jentezen pastors Free Chapel in Gainesville, Georgia, and Irvine, California. "When you release something precious to you, you enter into the dimension of the doubtless." Oh, really? (Source:https://www.youtube.com/watch?v=9rInjYXfI_4

Some famous Jentezen quotes:
"David put 5 stones in his bag, we would call it a purse, 5 is the number for grace, he put grace in his pocketbook. Grace was put into his finances." (Jentezen Franklin, TBN, Share-A-Thon)

"The Lord told me to tell you that 3,000 people that are watching, a miracle is about to begin again. Go to the phone now and say, 'I'm sowing a $55 seed.'" (Jentezen Franklin, TBN, Share-A-Thon)

"Some of your ministries are at a standstill, sow a $55 seed and see what God will do." (Jentezen Franklin, TBN, Share-A-Thon.

"Sow a $55 grace seed (Double Portion), some may criticize and not believe me. Well, just sit there. Some of you may get a blessing, but you won't get no money." (Jentezen Franklin, TBN, Share-A-Thon)

Jentezen has a 2.8-million-dollar condo in Florida. In Georgia, his home is worth over two million, and in California, his house was worth 2.2 million.

Jentezen later teamed up with another shameless heretic, Paula White, and was seen at many White House events during the Trump administration.

Carlton Pearson was once a protege of Oral Roberts. He attended ORU and was ordained with the Church of God in Christ. He pastored Higher Dimensions Church in Tulsa, Oklahoma, once attended by the late singer, Carman. Boasting of a congregation of 5000, the church faced foreclosure in 2006.

Carlton married Gina Marie Gauthier at the age of forty. While in Tulsa, Carlton declared there is no hell and began practicing Universalism and Ultimate Reconciliation, a belief that everyone gets saved whether they are born again or not. He lost his church, as people began leaving in droves, and he later moved to Chicago to pastor the New Age Christ Universal Temple. He never renounced his heresy, and he passed away in November 2023 of cancer.

Larry Huch, or Larry Huckster, and his wife show-me-the-money, Tiz. Another Stepford wife and she also is his partner in the "I love money more than anything" TV program.

Glossary of Other Miracle Sellers

Larry said, "Jesus is not the only begotten Son Of God!" His sidekick here is the evil Paula White. I guess he writes his own Bible. He also ignorantly mispronounces Hebrew words as he takes us back under the law, with a myriad of Jewish feast days that he says we are bound to celebrate. And we must always have some money in our hands. This man actually pastors a church in Irvine, Texas.
https://www.youtube.com/watch?v=E9aZH1sZ3Z0

In 2012 he declared in a sermon: "This will begin what we call the end-time transfer of wealth. And that when these Gentiles begin to receive this blessing, they will never go back financially through the valley again. They will grow and grow and grow. It's said this way: that God is looking at the church and everyone in it and deciding in the next three and a half years who will be his bankers. And the ones that say here I am Lord, you can trust me, we will become so blessed that we will usher in the coming of the Messiah."

https://www.youtube.com/watch?v=ZUsj3I4Uk44

Good thing that he did not live in Old Testament times; he'd be stoned!

Larry and Tiz own millions of dollars' worth of real estate, including a home valued at $3 million and a ranch.

Rick Joyner is now based at the old Heritage USA, or PTL in Fort Mill, North Carolina. It once belonged to Jim and Tammy Bakker. A friend from the internet lived there and said the most bizarre things went on. She ran for her life from the fanatical dancing and the endless prophesying, especially by the likes of Todd Bentley who has been accused of numerous perverted acts, as well as adultery. https://www.christianitytoday.com/2020/01/todd-bentley-charismatic-preacher-investigation-misconduct/

Here are some of Joyner's fantastic quotes, and, of course, he is special because he claims he goes to heaven.

"I was caught up in to heaven for eight hours........ I say prophetic, but I don't know if it was just a prophetic experience or if I was really there, but it seemed real. I saw things that I believe really are part of the heavenly realm.

"But this one was many times better than I'd ever experienced before. At the end of the whole dream - and this was an 8-hour, earth-time dream - I know because it started at midnight. I laid down at midnight, went right to sleep, went right into this dream, woke up several times during the night astonished, just trying to understand everything that I had just seen and heard. I'd then fall back to sleep and go right back into the same place. Over and over.... I'd had that experience one time before, just one time, where I woke up, and went back to the same place in the dream, but

this time it happened over and over. It was just awesome."
https://www.youtube.com/watch?v=8p4P6fLUg9Y

"Many Protestant and Reformed theologies not only hinder, but actually prohibit, Christians from knowing God's voice. These theologies can be traced to the extreme interpretation of the prime Reformation motto sola scriptura, which means 'Scripture alone.'"

"In the near future, the church will not be looking back at the first-century church with envy because of the great exploits of those days, but all will be saying that He certainly did save His best wine for last. The most glorious times in all of history have now come upon us. You who have dreamed of one day being able to talk with Peter, John, and Paul are going to be surprised to find that they have all been waiting to talk to you! You have been chosen to see the harvest, the fruit of the seeds that they were planting."

https://disntr.com/2021/04/01/the-dangers-of-false-prophet-rick-joyner-and-morningstar-ministries/

Rick suffered a stroke in 2023, which was a major setback for him. Chris Reed was appointed to serve as CEO and President of Morning Star Ministries in Fort Mill, South Carolina, to replace Rick.

Resigning in 2024, Chris said it was because of the many lawsuits that were filed against the ministry pertaining to alleged sexual assaults by a former volunteer. He stated he did not want to be a party to all of this and wanted to stand with the victims. After resigning, it was soon reported that Chris carried on a brief affair in 2021 with a student at Morning Star named Kathryn, sending her explicit sexual text messages and engaging in kissing, etc. Chris denies that there was intercourse. Even after all this, Rick gave Chris a major leadership role at the ministry. Now they are both accusing one another on various public platforms, and the war has begun. What a mess.

T.D. Jakes - Thomas Dexter Jakes is the man who talks and everyone supposedly listens, but he never really makes any sense to me.

He has become one of the most famous and sought-after speakers of the day, and don't mess with T.D. or else. Just ask David Lee, author of *Sunday Morning Stick-up: What your pastor doesn't want you to know about tithes*.

David, who knew T.D. as far back as his West Virginia days and was the national sales manager for Jakes, was at the Potter's House one Sunday morning as usual. And he was asked to leave. Why? Because his not-yet-released book telling the truth about "tithing" was a threat to T.D. and his false teachings on prosperity. God forbid people should find out what the Bible says on the subject of tithing, then these men would have to practice what they preach and live by faith!!

David Lee has been a guest on my internet radio program, Prophetic News Radio, so you can hear his testimony for yourself by going to my archived programs.

David was asked to surrender his ordination license which he held for twenty years and told he could no longer sit up front with the other elders and ministers. In other words, he received the scarlet letter and was shunned by Sheryl Brady (the pastor), who bankrupted her own church, The River in Durham, North Carolina. The property was foreclosed, and T.D. took her on in Texas. Mrs. Prosperity preacher, who flopped herself sowing seed faith gifts.

It was at Sheryl's branch in Parker, Texas, outside of Dallas at the illustrious "campus" where courses in sheep fleecing are held regularly, that the deed was done.

David Lee, Bible teacher and a true exponent of the-tithe-is-money lie, was further humiliated when, one Sunday while attending with his two small children, he was approached as he was sitting behind his designated pillar ten rows behind by four policemen. He was picked up and dragged out of the church while his little children cried, and oh, yes, Sheryl got the OK from God-is-love T.D. to revoke his license for telling the truth about tithing. Although they had never read the book, God forbid.

David never mentions their names in the book, so it is not about them. It is about the tithe was never money, but then again, T.D. and Sheryl don't like those scriptures, because then they would have to get real jobs, besides acting and lying about tithing. Once outside, David was told not to return, or he would be arrested. I wonder if T.D. and Sheryl are related to any of the Inquisitors from the 1500s?

T.D. inferred in an interview that David and Jonathan were homosexuals and maybe Ruth and Naomi were too. Raised in the Jesus-only movement, he still states that there is one God in three manifestations, not three persons. What?

"There is one God, Creator of all things, infinitely perfect, and eternally existing in three manifestations: Father, Son and Holy Spirit." As we can see, the "belief statement" on the Potter's House website still provides a Unitarian and distinctly Oneness concept of God. Using the term "manifestations" (thus avoiding the use of "Persons") to describe God is consistent with Oneness doctrine, not Trinitarianism.

https://jakesdivinity.org/about-jds/faith-statement/#:~:text=God.%20There%20is%20one%20God%2C%20Creator%20of,three%20manifestations:%20Father%2C%20Son%2C%20and%20Holy%20Spirit.

Here is another outrageous quote from Jakes:

"Ruth turns to Naomi and says 'I shall not leave thee.' She makes her statement to this woman... that sounds somewhat, somewhere in between poetry, intimacy, and borders on lesbianism. People don't even know how to explain what Ruth said to Naomi. It makes them uncomfortable. They're afraid to talk about it. They don't want to teach on it. Same thing with David and Jonathan... where there were same-sex relationships getting too close, people don't even know what to say." https://www.youtube.com/watch?v=CZkUTR-oKMo

And why was Jakes wearing an earring to his daughter's first wedding? I saw the photo, and it was later doctored to erase the diamond stud from the aforementioned ear. Very strange.

He even requires a tithe from people who join his ministerial fellowship. PHIPA or The Potters House International Pastoral Alliance, it is part of the covenant that you make to rub shoulders with T.D.'s name. Another reason to throw David Lee under the bus. The tithe must come from the pastor's salary, according to the Jakes' website.

In 2013, Oprah Winfrey was a speaker at his Mega-Fest conference. Oprah is not a Christian, and she promotes demonic New Age beliefs and practices. Tyler Perry gave Jakes one million dollars and oh, yes, he's a "Christian," yet he had a baby with his girlfriend. Tyler could write and produce great movie scripts, but his movies do not reflect holiness. He could be a great influence on the young if he truly followed Christian principles.

T.D. and his cronies have their own form of Christianity; it is not Bible-based. When you make the cover of *Time* magazine as a Christian leader, you have not arrived, because Jesus said in his own words that YOU would be hated for His namesake.

According to the testimony of Jacob Morales, who was formerly employed by Ron Luce of Teen Mania, T.D. required a $100,000 speaking fee, the presidential suite at the hotel, a private jet, and many other perks just to speak for fifty minutes!

Although *Teen Mania* was having huge financial problems, here is a quote from an article about Ron Luce and T.D.

"Help, help, we're going under, yet we're dropping $100,000 for a guy who is going to speak for 50 minutes."

That payment, Morales said, went to Dallas minister T.D. Jakes to get him to speak at a New York City Battle Cry event on Feb. 8, 2008. (Jennifer Saunier, then *Teen Mania*'s sales director, confirmed that figure; Jake's organization did not respond to a request for comment.)

Morales says *Teen Mania* chartered a $21,000 private jet and spent more than $4,000 on a two-night stay at the Ritz Carlton for Jakes, whom Luce wanted as a *Teen Mania* partner. Morales says he had discretion over $10,000 in cash to buy imported flowers, chocolates, rare bread, candy, iPods, and other gifts for the Jakes family to find in their hotel suite,

Glossary of Other Miracle Sellers

green room, and two Cadillac Escalade limousines.
https://www.lipstickalley.com/threads/teen-mania-paid-td-jakes-140-000-for-50-min.705989/

There are other much more serious issues with T.D. Jakes that were reported recently in the Christian Post. Jakes brought a lawsuit against Duane Youngblood for defamation as Youngblood accused Jakes of trying to molest him many years ago. Youngbloods brother Richard then joined a countersuit claiming that Jakes did sexually assault him in a sworn affidavit , it allegedly happened in the fall of 1990. There have been rumors for years concerning Jakes alleged homosexuality, but it has yet to be proven. Here is a link to the story.
https://www.christianpost.com/news/brother-of-td-jakes-accuser-says-pastor-tried-to-assult-him.html

I believe God, in His time, will bring the house of Jakes crashing down!

Potter's House Church has a congregation of well over eleven thousand. Jakes enjoys very expensive real estate to the tune of over ten million. His house sits on seventeen acres and is over 14,000 sq. ft. in Texas.

Jesse Duplantis: Jesse is a prosperity man, who also has a testimony of going to heaven. He claims he talks to dead people, which is forbidden by the Word of God; that is necromancy.

"When thou art come into the land which the LORD thy God giveth thee, thou shalt not learn to do after the abominations of those nations.
There shall not be found among you anyone that maketh his son or his daughter to pass through the fire, or that useth divination, or an observer of times, or an enchanter or a witch,
Or a charmer, or a consulter with familiar spirits or a wizard, or a necromancer.
For all that do these things are an abomination unto the LORD: and because of

Glossary of Other Miracle Sellers

these abominations the LORD thy God doth drive them out from before thee." Deuteronomy 18

But Jesse knows the Word!! He is rich, and some of it comes from the pyramid scheme of collecting tithe money. No faith or grace is involved there. Yet Jesse is a Word man, but he never really read the scriptures concerning tithing, or did he read them and still continues to lie?

Jesse just built the biggest house in Louisiana, over thirty thousand square feet or so; he said one of the chandeliers was worth over a million dollars. He loves to brag. Here are some famous Jesse quotes from sermons and television appearances.

"If I give 1,000 dollars, I deserve to get back $100,000. That's not greed!"

"The Lord spoke to me one time while I was preachin, he said to make me laugh, how do you make God laugh, Benny? (speaking to

Benny Hinn) he said the gift that I gave you let it come out of you, so I said OK so I began to minister and I tell you what I have made God laugh. Many, many times."

"One time the funniest was I'm embarrassed to say this, this is when I first started preaching, I knew enough to be dangerous you know how that is. We didn't stay in hotels in those days, stayed in people's homes...! got this apartment, I got this bedroom and I always take my Bible before I go to sleep... when anyway I fell off to sleep with the Bible hit me on the chest and I woke up and there's this big gray object in the corner and it would move.

"That scared me but I wasn't getting off that bed, I said no I ain't getting off this bed, I said I rebuke you, you devil from hell get out of here, get out of here. I spit and hollered and screamed and rebuked all until 5, 5:30 till my throat was hoarse. And the light began to come through the window, and it was a raincoat hangin' over a hat rack. I can't

believe I that I actually rebuked the raincoat for 3 hours. Now here's the funny part I got mad at God, I said why didn't you tell me? He said 'Jesse that's the funniest thing I ever saw. Rebuking a raincoat boy.'"
https://www.youtube.com/watch?v=-CwjeSFhi-M

"He (God) didn't have the foggiest idea what a horse was, he said maybe Adam might know what this is. He is made in my image and my likeness let's see what he says it is, because he has a speaking spirit just like God the speaking spirit. He brought them, that means he carried them... what do you call that Adam, do you see that he brought them? He didn't say horsy get down the road and trot down there and find out what your name is, bird fly down there ... no they're not living. God is expecting Adam to do the same thing he did, 'speak spirit!'
http://www.letusreason.org/WF54.htm

"Women's seed spoke just as God spoke Adam into existence, as Adam spoke those animals into existence. Mary spoke Jesus into existence. Don't tell me a woman cannot preach the gospel they got Jesus here without us."

https://www.youtube.com/watch?v=2yhTxaTfC9M

James Robison: He went to Rome to kiss the ring of "Pope" Francis. He was photographed high-fiving Bergoglio. Please, I can't take any more. Now we must cavort with the Whore of Babylon, all in the name of unity. James has gone-a-whoring with the rest of the false prophets and false teachers. His ministry recently took in sixty-eight million dollars, and spent less than ten million on missions.

Fort Worth, TX
Founded: 1963
Tel: (817) 267-4211
Website: http://www.lifetoday.org
Top Leader: Rev. James Robison
Donor Contact: Rep. Donor Assistance
Member Since: 11/17/1993

- Financial Data	
Revenue:	
Cash Donations:	$65,060,955
Noncash Donations:	$0

James enjoys the use of a private jet and a million-dollar-plus home in Texas.

Chuck Missler: Now deceased. If you like aliens and Nephilim, then Chuck is your man. Of course, they cannot explain the fact that fallen angels do not have blood, so how can they father children? They also do not have the body parts, since they are spirits, but gullible Christians buy his fantasies.

Here are some quotes from Missler about secret codes in the Bible!

His book *is Cosmic Codes, Hidden Messages from the Edge of Eternity.*

"Some [codes], we discover are hidden behind, or underneath, our day-to-day traffic of ideas. The ones which are hidden usually reveal an ulterior intent or purpose.... From the ancient palaces of our earliest cultures to the super-secret 'black chambers' of our most modern command posts, the art of secret writing and the science of their decipherment have determined the course of history.

Cryptology - the study of secret codes and ciphers- has also been stimulated by its use in literature."

We do not need hidden or secret codes in the Bible! Missler also has plagiarized some of his books and has since apologized. Here is an example.
"...there is evidence to suggest that our world and everything in it are also only ghostly images, projections from a level of reality so beyond our own it is literally beyond both space and time."
~ New Age author Michael Talbot, 1991

"...there is evidence to suggest that our world and everything in it are also only ghostly images, projections from a level of reality so beyond our own it is literally beyond both space and time."
~ Christian author Chuck Missler, 1999

This link here will take you to their website. Sarah Leslie and Gaylene Goodroad http://www.herescope.blogspot.com.

Their scholarly research will keep you well-informed on church matters.

Kim Clement: He claims he heard an audible word from the Lord when he was baptized, and ya know, everyone who hears the audible voice of God becomes a prophet. Kim wanted you to know that he was special.

Here are some infamous quotes of Kim from many sermons and television appearances.

"I thought that Christianity was based on a relationship resulting from grace. My idea that each person is born with a treasure in their spirit is mocked, and I am accused of being a new age prophet because I will NOT focus on their sin but rather on their treasure...I know how a sinner feels because I have been one...I do not believe that you must be born again to obtain salvation....you cannot and will not make a disciple out of a sinner who has been introduced to Jesus Christ on the basis of their sinful inheritance only."

"I'm telling you there's going to be some ignoramuses coming to meetings, into our meetings, the New Millennium church, that's not focusing on the sin and trying to force them to repent and make them afraid because they're going to go to hell."
https://bigchurch.com/blog/174/post_4594.html?passthru_override=1DDDD

"When you're born again the Bible doesn't say that you are saved. The Bible says that when you are born again you see the kingdom it doesn't say that you are saved even though salvation takes place and rebirth causes you to see the kingdom of God."
https://www.lavistachurchofchrist.org/cms/have-you-heard-about-kim-clement/

"You cannot and will not make a disciple out of a sinner who has been introduced to Jesus Christ on the basis of their sinful inheritance only. The sinner wants something that he does not have. To approach them the way Jesus approached the sinner was through His perception of their need and the potential that was inside of them.

"Approach them on the basis of their sin and condemning them to Hell, will only increase their contempt or will manipulate them into making a decision in order to survive the flames of Hell. Although we know that hell is a reality and sin is their snare, the way Jesus approached the sinner was through His perception of their need and the potential that was inside of them."

Kim also has come out with some whoppers about Pope Francis.

"I speak of the one who calls himself after St. Francis of Assisi. The Spirit of the Lord spoke for him to come and stand at the head, but this man is not like any other, says the Lord. This man has been appointed to join the hearts of the Protestant faith and Catholic and those who are Spirit-filled. And I will do something so unique and so different, says the Lord, because of his acknowledgment of My power.

"And I have chosen Pope Francis as one of the voices that will speak, and he will command and they will try and assassinate him three times. They will try within to damage him. God says they will even try to poison him, but his voice will not be stopped, says the Lord. I will cause people to run to the cross, people to cling to the cross. Many souls shall come. And then, God says, there will be a change in the entire system. I will make a change, for what Martin Luther did 500 years ago, and when he nailed a thesis to the door and said, 'This is it - we believe that by faith we are saved, which is a gift of God, saved unto works, not by works.' God's Spirit says so it shall be that this man shall pronounce that as well and there shall be fire that shall ignite in the southern part of America, in the central part of America.
https://www.youtube.com/watch?v=xW98msbJqOk

Kim, like the other false prophets and teachers, tries to push unity with Rome. This is a big red flag for all of us. Kim recently suffered two strokes and had a brain bleed. He needed brain surgery and was recovering in a rehab facility. Later, Kim passed away in December 2016. He was sixty years old.

Clarence McClendon: Clarence has been seen on the TV program, *Preachers of LA*, where he flaunted his wealth and his "anointing." All of it was questionable. Clarence was also a TBN favorite because he comes up with the wildest stories about God and the "Holy Spirit" and how they want to access your bank account in order to bless you by blessing him.

Clarence dumped his first wife, Tammera, for an updated model, Priscilla, reportedly marrying her just seven days after his divorce.

Clarence claims he was "called" at an early age. Hey, Clarence, we are all called. Ever heard of "Go ye into all the world and preach the gospel"? God is no respecter of persons! You are not special.

Here are some famous Clarence quotes from his many telethon and preaching engagements.

"God spoke to me that there are 1,000 people that will give no less than $100, I got this word! Get up! Get up! Get up! Go to the phone. The Spirit of God promised me that He would bless your seed! Go to the phone right now! If you're sowing $1,000, do it now! If you're sowing $100, do it now."

"Some of you are wrestling with debt that you cannot pay off. God told me this morning to tell you to take that credit card, God spoke expressly in my spirit, for you to sow a seed on the credit card that you want God to pay off, God said, 'let me touch that situation.' God said, 'to tell them to put it on the card, and in 30 days they can deal with the debt and pay it off,' I am speaking a prophetic word right now...Get Jesus on that credit card, make a pledge on that credit card."

Yeah, a "prophetic" word from your god, the devil! It was not our Jesus because He never talked like that. Clarence enjoys a $7.5-million-dollar home in California among many other benefits derived from his false prosperity gospel.

Eddie Long: Oh, Eddie, what were you thinking when you sent the photos of yourself to those young men you were accused of molesting? Eddie was sued by four young men accusing him of using them for sex. Anyway, Eddie protested his innocence, but he settled the lawsuit OUT of court. So, if you are innocent, why pay hush money?

One young man, Spencer LeGrande, *e*ven wrote a book, "Foursaken: The Long Road to forgiveness." Yet Eddie still had a following at New Birth there in Lithonia, Georgia, outside of Atlanta. According to public records, his house was in foreclosure at the time, but yet, "Apostle" Long announced he was holding a conference in Florida, believe it or not!

"Join Apostle Eddie L. Long for the 2015 Kingdom Power Glory Summit 'Catch the Revelation,' September 8-10, 2015, at the Diplomat Resort and Spa in Greater Fort Lauderdale, Florida.

You will receive revelatory knowledge and tools on how to fulfill your God-given purpose in the Kingdom and Marketplace.

"'Don't miss this amazing opportunity for you to meet your needs.' Long says his luxury cars are 'side benefits of saying yes to God.' Money isn't evil; the love of money is evil. Pastors need to show people 'visual sermons' to demonstrate that God is blessing them, he says."

Long even warned those who might look for flaws in their pastor: People who disrespect their leaders not only disobey God, they bring harm onto themselves, he says.

"Once the flock of God leaves the green grass and clear water of God's presence to gnaw on their shepherds," he writes, "their insurrection kills their blessing and aborts their corporate victory." (Quote from a CNN article published in October 2010)

Eddie was also involved with convicted con artist Ephren Taylor. Members of his church who were defrauded settled a lawsuit with Long.

Long had endorsed Taylor to New Birth Missionary Baptist Church congregants as his "friend" and "brother" during a financial seminar in October 2009. Taylor managed to convince members to invest nearly a million dollars into ventures that were essentially nonexistent.

Long died of an aggressive form of cancer in January 2017 at the age of sixty-three, a shell of his former self.

The funeral was bizarre. He was laid out in the church wearing what looked like a Catholic bishop outfit in red, white, and gold. Most of the other ministers were either dressed like Catholic priests in black suits and Roman collars, or they also wore the Catholic bishop's outfits.

His New Birth church has now been taken over by Jamal Bryant, who was also made famous as a miracle seller on the TBN Network.

Epilogue

There are so many false teachers and false prophets, they could fill over a thousand pages. A sad commentary about the state of Christianity today.

And what is the moral of the story? Run from heretics. Flee for your life from false teachers. Serve God with all your heart. Give out of love, not for selfish motives.

Let the Reformation begin in you as we say no to the seed faith, miracle-selling gospel. No more!!

And finally, my article on Seed Faith published in 1997:

The Error of Seed Faith Giving

I began to notice something was happening to the Body of Christ that was having devastating consequences and causing incredible selfishness, and its source was the very popular teaching of sowing seed or seed faith.

Selfishness: caring only or chiefly for self; regarding one's own interest chiefly or solely, proceeding from love of self, influenced in actions solely by a view to private advantage. (Webster's dictionary)

Sow a seed and meet "your" need violates the commandment Jesus left with us in Matthew 22:37-40:

"Thou shalt love the Lord thy God with all thy heart, and all thy soul, and with all thy mind. This is the first and great commandment and the second is like unto it. Thou shalt LOVE thy neighbor as thyself. On these two commandments hang all the law and the prophets."

When our motive in giving is selfishness, for our own gain, we disregard the fact that the New Testament is based on love. Love gives!

Love never fails! Without love, we are nothing.

> *"God's love seeketh not her own."*
> *1 Corinthians 13*

God so loved the world that He gave.

To love our neighbor as ourselves would be to see a need and to meet that need. (Not sow a seed and meet "our" need.) I cannot find any scripture that associates money with "seed." "Seed" is the Word of God.

> *"Being born again not of corruptible seed, but incorruptible by the Word of God."*
> *1 Peter 1:23*

Seed is "sperma," agricultural and botanical or offspring (Vines Greek dictionary). If you sow money in the ground, you will not get a harvest! You cannot buy God's blessings! God Almighty is not moved by dollar bills. Some preachers will say, "Sow $100 and God will give you a miracle or buy you a husband or a wife. Need a healing, how about $1,000 seed?" The bigger the seed, the bigger the miracle. What nonsense!

God doesn't need money; we do! God does not have money in heaven that He drops out of the sky. His exchange is faith, believing that when you pray, He answers.

> *"But Peter said unto him, thy money perish with thee because thou hast thought that the Gift of God may be purchased with money. Thou has neither part nor lot in this matter, for thy heart is not right in the sight of God. Repent, therefore, of this thy wickedness and pray God, if perhaps the thought of thine heart be forgiven thee."*
> *Acts 8:20-22*

The gift of the working of miracles is a free gift. The gift of healing is free! I heard one preacher say she sowed a $1,000 seed for her daughter's healing to prophet so-and-so (false prophet). I don't care what prophet so-and-so said. I care what Prophet Jesus said!

Epilogue

"Forasmuch as ye know that ye were not redeemed with incorruptible things, as silver and gold. But with the precious blood of Christ."
1 Peter 1:1

When your child has a need, sometimes you see the need and meet it without them asking. When was the last time your child said to you, "Mom and Dad, if I give you five dollars, would you love me; would you feed me; would you bless me?" No, and our loving Heavenly Father does not behave that way either.

"Or what man is there of you whom if his son ask for bread, will he give him a stone? Or if he ask for a fish will give him a serpent? If ye then being evil know how to give good gifts unto your children, how much more shall your Father which is in heaven give good things to them that ASK Him?"
Matthew 7:9-11

I believe give and it shall be given, but I also believe "it is more blessed to give than to receive." (Read Acts 20:35.) In the Gospel of Luke 11:42, Jesus rebuked the Pharisees when they bragged about their tithing. He didn't say, "Nice little Pharisees, you gave [or sowed a seed], so I must bless you."

Jesus said, "But woe unto you Pharisees! For ye tithe mint and rue and all manner of herbs, and pass over judgment and the Love of God. These ought ye to have done and not to leave the other undone."

Go on, Jesus! (Notice tithing was food, not money, as most "FAITH" preachers want you to believe. They do not live by faith, but by 10%!!) I have never seen one scripture that refers to tithing as money.

"Woe unto you scribes and Pharisees, hypocrites! For ye make clean the outside of the cup and of the platter, but within they are full of extortion and excess."
Matthew 23:25

Sow your seed and meet your need? No, not out of necessity, but because you love your neighbor as yourself! I taught another gospel, and I was wrong, and I am not saying all the preachers who teach this are wicked, but they are misinformed. I had to repent, and if you find yourself in this error, repent. Study to show yourself approved and go on and be a blessing to the people Jesus died for!

"Brethren, if any of you do err from the truth and one convert him, let him know that he which converteth the sinner from the error of his way shall save a soul from death and shall hide a multitude of sins."
James 5:20

"We are of God; he that knoweth God heareth us; he that is not of God heareth not us. Hereby know we the Spirit of Truth and the Spirit of Error."
1 John 4:6

Prayer to be born again and to receive Jesus Christ as your Lord and Savior:

"Dear Lord Jesus, I know that I am a sinner, and I ask for your forgiveness. I believe you died for my sins and rose from the dead. I will trust and follow You as my Lord and Savior. Take my life and help me to do your will. In Jesus' name, amen."

We cannot earn salvation; it is a free gift.

We are saved by God's grace when we have faith in His Son, Jesus Christ. You must acknowledge that you are a sinner, that Christ died for your sins, and ask for His forgiveness. Then turn from your sins; that's called repentance, heartfelt repentance.

"He that believeth and is baptized shall be saved; but he that believeth not shall be damned."
Mark 16:16

"Then Peter said unto them, Repent, and be baptized every one of you in the name of Jesus Christ for the remission of sins, and ye shall receive the gift of the Holy Ghost."
Acts 2:38

"That if thou shalt confess with thy mouth the Lord Jesus, and shalt believe in thine heart that God hath raised him from the dead, thou shalt be saved."
Romans 10:9

"And now why tarriest thou? arise, and be baptized, and wash away thy sins, calling on the name of the Lord."
Acts 22:16

"For God so loved the world, that he gave his only begotten Son, that whosoever believeth in him should not perish, but have everlasting life."
John 3:16-17

"For by grace are ye saved through faith; and that not of yourselves: [it is] the gift of God:"
Ephesians 2:8-9

"But God commendeth his love toward us, in that, while we were yet sinners, Christ died for us."
Romans 5:8

"Neither is there salvation in any other: for there is none other name under heaven given among men, whereby we must be saved."
Acts 4:12

Acknowledgments

To Almighty God for His Word, and we will forever thank Him for sending Jesus, our Savior!!

Thanks to Barry Bowen of the Trinity Foundation for providing some of the housing information.

Ministry Watch for salary information.

End Notes

Chapter 4

Ashes to Gold, Patti Roberts, Jove Publications 1987

CNN.com, October 16, 2007

Gimme that Prime Time Religion, 1979, Jerry Sholes, p. 8

Chapter 5

D.R. McConnell, *A Different Gospel*, p. 64

Preface: *A Different Gospel*, D.R. McConnell

Hagin vs. Kenyon comparisons

Ruth Kenyon Houseworth, 1982 taped interview, Lynnwood, WA, Feb. 19, 1982

The Hidden Man, E.W. Kenyon, 1910, p. 40

A Different Gospel, D.R. McConnell, p. 69

Kenneth Hagin's testimony, "I Went to Hell" on YouTube and in his book.

https://youtu.be/KdicUqbcs4U?si=SbpjufkSZhu8re3t

A Different Gospel, D.R. McConnell, p. 75,

Chapter 9

Orange County Register, June 8, 2012

Wikipedia: August 30, 2011

Brittany Crouch Koper interview, Orange County Register

Jackie Alnor's interview with Brittany Crouch

https://youtu.be/8lY2ygUXWpc?si=Q8aKTa_Dfh2W498h

Chapter 10

United States Copyright law, Wikipedia

http://www.usatoday.com/story/opinion/2015/09/01/donald-trump-evangelical-votercolumn/71482794/

Tampa Bay Business Journal, Pam Huff

Lakeland Ledger, Gary White, March 16, 2014

Credit Union Times, Michelle Samaad, June 26, 2014

End Notes

Bankruptcy Filing, Without Walls Church United States Bankruptcy Court, April 20, 2014

gov.uscourts.flmb.1136819.54.0.pdf

Paula White and Jonathan Cain watch porn

https://www.youtube.com/watch?v=UMbXrL7q1zU

Chapter 11

Juanita Bynum:

https://readychurch.wordpress.com/2013/11/16/juanita-bynum-now-with-gandhi-hinduismbuddhism-confucianism-religions/

Chapter 12

The Buffington Post, February 26, 2014

Chapter 13

Kenneth Copeland Ministers Conference, 2014

Wikipedia: William Tyndale

Wikipedia: History of the Bible

A Different Gospel, D.R. McConnell, p.118

Kenneth Copeland, The Power of the Resurrection

https://www.kcm.org/real-help/healing/speak/10-confessions-activate-resurrection-power-god-your-life?language_content_entity=en-US

Council of Trent, 1545-1563, Bologna, Italy

Kenneth Copeland Ministers conference, January 2014, quote from Pope Francis

End Notes

The Bull Cantate Domino, 1441

https://catholicism.org/cantate-domino.html

Quote from Pope Francis, 2013

https://wdtprs.com/2013/04/pope-francis-it-is-not-possible-to-find-jesus-outside-the-church/

Chapter 14

"Empty Suit Preacher Sinks Illinois Church":

https://www.salon.com/2013/03/05/indiana_mega_church_faces_foreclosure_partner/

https://www.nwitimes.com/news/local/lake/article_534a436a-e367-54d3-9fc1-716f844624d3.html

February 1, 2013

Chapter 16

Daystar Television Network, Wikipedia

Marcus Lamb quotes from Daystar Television archives

Chapter 17

Paul Crouch quotes: From TBN television archives

Chapter 19

Wikipedia: TCT Television Network

Chapter 21

Wikipedia: Morris Cerullo

The End time Manifestation of the Sons of God, Morris Cerullo

https://youtu.be/w8SdEaMfRIc?si=bFLrAB OiJuXaaZsW

End Notes

The Legacy Center Brochure, San Diego, California

Wikipedia: Inspiration Ministries

http://www.pfo.org/NewsUpdatesIndex.html

David Lee, The book-Sunday Morning Stickup available on Amazon

T.D. Jakes on Oneness

http://www.christiandefense.org/Oneness TD%20Takes%20Update.html

Sarah Leslie and Gaylene Goodroad, Herescope Blog, Chuck Missler

https://herescope.net/2013/08/without-attribution.html

Kim Clement quotes

Kim Clement's ongoing prophetic Promises

Nine of the Richest Pastors in America

1. Kenneth Copeland: over $750 million
2. Joel Osteen: $50 million
   Donations are said to total over $40 million a year.
3. Benny Hinn: estimated $40-60 million
4. Steven Furtick: $60 million
   According to ECFA, his church, Elevation, has a net worth of over $319 million.
5. Andy Stanley: $40 million
6. Creflo Dollar: $28 million
7. Rick Warren: $25 million
8. T.D. Jakes: estimated at $150 million
9. Churches in Africa and United States David Oyedepo has a net worth of $150 Million
   10

These totals may fluctuate, as there are a few websites with different totals. This is personal wealth. (Source: Ministry Watch)

Twenty-two of the Largest Churches in America

Life Church, Craig Groeschel: 60,000

Church of the Highlands, Chris Hodges: 60,000

Christ's Church of the Valley, Ashley Woolridge: 48,000

Lakewood Church, Joel Osteen: 45,000

North Point Ministries, Andy Stanley: 43,000

Christ Fellowship Church, Todd Mullins: 32,000

Saddleback Church, Andy Wood: 30,000

Crossroads Church, Brian Tome: 27,000

Eagle Brook Church, Jason Strand: 25,000

Southeast Christian Church, Kyle Idleman: 25,000

Fellowship Church, Ed Young: 25,000

Harvest Christian Fellowship, Greg Laurie: 20,000

Second Baptist Church, Edwin Young: 19,000

Prestonwood Baptist Church, Jack Graham: 19,000

Elevation Church, Steven Furtick: 17,000

King Jesus International Ministry, Guillermo Maldonado: 16,000

Dream City Church, Luke Barnett: 15,000

Abundant Church, Charles Nieman: 14,000

Jentezen Franklin Free Chapel: 13,000

New Light Church, Irishea Hilliard: 13,000

World Changers, Creflo Dollar: 13,000

Family Christian Center, Steve Munsey: 13,000

Salaries of Ministry Executives 2021 or 2022

David Cerullo $4.5 million

Chuck Pierce $2,084,437

Tony Evans $1,407,218

Cindy Trimm $984,549

Franklin Graham $832,738

Mathew Crouch $829,697

Jo Lynn Lindsey $750,000

Edgar Sandoval World Vision $556,341

Pat Robertson $572,094

David Jeremiah $472,690

Susan is also the author of

Paula White: President Trump's Pastor

A biography of the real Paula White

Website:www.propheticnews.com

https://heretics.propheticnews.com/

YouTube channel
Prophetic News TV

https://www.youtube.com/@SusanPuzio-propheticnewstv

Susan on X

https://x.com/SusanPuzio007

contact Susan by email

propheticnewstv@gmail.com

or

susan@propheticnews.com

The Miracle Sellers

www.ingramcontent.com/pod-product-compliance
Lightning Source LLC
LaVergne TN
LVHW051823080426
835512LV00018B/2696